GARDEN PONDS
A QUARTERLY

by John Coborn

yearBOOKS,INC.
Dr. Herbert R. Axelrod,
   Founder & Chairman
Neal Pronek
   Chief Editor

T.F.H. yearBOOKS and Quarterlies are all photo composed, color separated and designed on Scitex equipment in Neptune, N.J. with the following staff:

COMPUTER ART
   Michael L. Secord
      Supervisor
   Sherise Buhagiar
   Patti Escabi
   Cynthia Fleureton
   Sandra Taylor Gale
   Pat Marotta
   Joanne Muzyka
   Robert Onyrscuk

Advertising Sales
George Campbell
   Chief
Amy Manning
   Coordinator

©yearBOOKS,Inc.
1 TFH Plaza
Neptune, N.J.07753

Completely manufactured in Neptune, N.J. USA

Although more people than ever are now deciding to have a pond on their home property, this is certainly not a modern innovation. It was probably the ancient Chinese who first got ponds off to a fine art thousands of years ago and they even developed special colorful varieties of fish, notably goldfish, to populate them. The Chinese initiative was followed by the Japanese, who are masters at incorporating artificial bodies of water into their landscapes. They developed further varieties of goldfish and, of course, pioneered the fabulous varieties of Koi carp. It is reasonable to suppose that water features were included in the Hanging Gardens of Babylon and it is a known fact that Queen Hatshepsut of ancient Egypt cultivated lotus and papyrus at Luxor (c. 1480 BC).

Landscaped pools of one sort or another are now to be found in all parts of the world and most modern architectural developments include at least one water feature. The trend is for modern hotels and holiday resorts to have water features in front of or inside their entrance foyers and some remarkable constructions are to be seen in such places.

This text has been written as an introduction to the art of water gardening, and the information contained in the following pages will enable the beginner to start from scratch and create a living pool of his own.

What are Quarterlies?
Books, the usual way information of this sort is transmitted, can be too slow. Sometimes by the time a book is written and published, the material contained therein is a year or two old...and no new material has been added during that time. Only a book in a magazine form can bring breaking stories and current information. A magazine is streamlined in production, so we have adopted certain magazine publishing techniques in the creation of this Quarterly. Magazines also can be much cheaper than books because they are supported by advertising. To combine these assets into a great publication, we issued this Quarterly in both magazine and book format at different prices.

CUSTOMARY U.S. MEASURES AND EQUIVALENTS

LENGTH

1 inch (in)		= 2.54 cm
1 foot (ft)	= 12 in	= .3048 m
1 yard (yd)	= 3 ft	= .9144 m
1 mile (mi)	= 1760 yd	= 1.6093 km
1 nautical mile	= 1.152 mi	= 1.853 km

AREA

1 square inch (in^2)		= 6.4516 cm^2	
1 square foot (ft^2)	= 144 in^2	= .093 m^2	
1 square yard (yd^2)		= 9 ft^2	= .8361 m^2
1 acre	= 4840 yd^2	= 4046.86 m^2	
1 square mile(mi^2)		= 640 acre	= 2.59 km^2

WEIGHT

1 ounce (oz)	= 437.5 grains	= 28.35 g
1 pound (lb)	= 16 oz	= .4536 kg
1 short ton	= 2000 lb	= .9072 t
1 long ton	= 2240 lb	= 1.0161 t

VOLUME

1 cubic inch (in^3)		= 16.387 cm^3
1 cubic foot (ft^3)	= 1728 in^3	= .028 m^3
1 cubic yard (yd^3)	= 27 ft^3	= .7646 m^3
1 fluid ounce (fl oz)		= 2.957 cl
1 liquid pint (pt)	= 16 fl oz	= .4732 l
1 liquid quart (qt)	= 2 pt	= .946 l
1 gallon (gal)	= 4 qt	= 3.7853 l
1 dry pint		= .5506 l
1 bushel (bu)	= 64 dry pt	= 35.2381 l

METRIC MEASURES AND EQUIVALENTS

LENGTH

1 millimeter (mm)		= .0394 in
1 centimeter (cm)	= 10 mm	= .3937 in
1 meter (m)	= 1000 mm	= 1.0936 yd
1 kilometer (km)	= 1000 m	= .6214 mi

AREA

1 sq centimeter (cm^2)	= 100 mm^2	= .155 in^2
1 sq meter (m^2)	= 10,000 cm^2	= 1.196 yd^2
1 hectare (ha)	= 10,000 m^2	= 2.4711 acres
1 sq kilometer (km^2)	= 100 ha	= .3861 mi^2

WEIGHT

1 milligram (mg)		= .0154 grain
1 gram (g)	= 1000 mg	= .0353 oz
1 kilogram (kg)	= 1000 g	= 2.2046 lb
1 tonne (t)	= 1000 kg	= 1.1023 short tons
1 tonne	= .9842 long ton	

VOLUME

1 cubic centimeter (cm^3)	= .061 in^3	
1 cubic decimeter (dm^3)	= 1000 cm^3	= .353 ft^3
1 cubic meter (m^3)	= 1000 dm^3	= 1.3079 yd^3
1 liter (l)	= 1 dm^3	= .2642 gal
1 hectoliter (hl)	= 100 l	= 2.8378 bu

TEMPERATURE

$$\text{CELSIUS}° = 5/9 \ (\text{F}° - 32°) \quad \text{FAHRENHEIT}° = 9/5 \ \text{C}° + 32°$$

CONTENTS

There is almost nothing in this world that is as beautiful and peaceful as water falling into a garden pond in which colorful fishes are swimming. Photo by Bildarchiv Sammer.

POND SITING AND DESIGN

Before deciding to have a garden pond, one should bear in mind that it requires a certain amount of maintenance. A neglected pond can be much worse than no pond at all, so before one decides to take the initial step of installing, ensure that one has the ongoing enthusiasm to keep it as an attractive focal point of the garden. Having decided that a garden pond is for you, the first and most important point to consider is its location. It is possible, within reason, to construct a pond of some type in almost any location but, if you want to keep your maintenance to a minimum, there are a few important points to bear in mind. For the best results, the pond should be situated in a sunny site, but with part of the surface shaded; it should be sheltered as much as possible from prevailing winds but, at the same time, should not be too near to large trees, particularly deciduous varieties.

The pond must receive an adequate amount of sunlight, or the growth of the aquatic plants will be severely affected and the foliage they produce may be pale, stunted, and straggly. The ideal site is one which receives sunlight on half of its surface for most of the day. It should be protected to a certain extent against severe weather conditions; strong, cold winds can be a danger to both plants and fish. It is best, therefore, to site your pond in an area sheltered from prevailing winds by a fence, a wall or a hedge. If you do not have such a protective screen already available, you can perhaps erect a hedge or fence especially for that purpose.

Large trees near to a pond can pose several dangers.

and fish. In addition, the foliage, fruits, or branches of certain trees such as yew, laburnum, or pine can themselves be poisonous, releasing dangerous toxic oils into the water.

The ideal situation for your pond may also be influenced

A garden pond serves many purposes. It can be a beautiful guard against trespassers as well as a catch basin for areas in which rainwater accumulates. Photo by Dr. Herbert R. Axelrod.

Some trees develop extremely long root systems which can penetrate through the walls of the pond, causing serious damage which is not easy to repair. The leaves of both deciduous and coniferous trees falling into the water will soon foul it unless they are constantly removed. Large numbers of rotting leaves in the base of the pond will produce poisonous gases which can kill both plants

by the design you have in mind. Natural looking ponds of random shape are normally placed in a low-lying area of the garden, while those in which a series of ponds and waterfalls are envisaged will require a certain amount of sloping ground. One advantage of situating a pond on a higher area is that it is easy to drain out by siphoning with a hose. Formal ponds, perhaps with a fountain, are often best placed in a central position, arranged symmetrically among paths and flower beds, while an informal pond can be set in almost any part or corner. Some enthusiasts like their pond to be near to the house, where it can easily be viewed from a window. Such ponds are often part of the general design of the house and its surrounds, perhaps as part of a patio or incorporated near the entrance porch. If building a new house and you want a pond to be near to it, it is a good idea to have your architect include the pond in the initial plan. This is preferable to having to make alterations later on. There is really no right or wrong place to site a pond although some sites will be better than others and you may have to change your initial ideas somewhat, depending on the type of site available. However, even those sites which, at first, seem most unsuitable, can usually be adapted for your purposes.

In some areas, local building legislation may exist with regard to pond construction, so ensure that you have the necessary planning approval before embarking on an expensive project. For example, a fence may be required to protect the safety of small children in the area; it may be necessary to check that your pond is not situated

over access to sewers, water pipes, or electricity supplies; ponds situated on unstable ground can be dangerous. Great care should be taken if a pond is to be constructed

If huge stones are available, they can be used to surround a pond and make an exceptionally beautiful garden pond. These huge stones are available for sales worldwide and they are not as expensive as you might think. Photo by Dr. Herbert R. Axelrod.

behind a retaining wall, remembering that large bodies of water are extremely heavy and additional reinforcing may be required.

Another factor which may affect your selection of a site may be the availability of

water, both for the initial filling and the regular topping up of water lost by evaporation. If possible, it is best to have a water outlet near to the pond, rather than have to unroll endless lengths of hosepipe every time you require to top it up, clean the surroundings, etc. An additional water tap in the area will come in handy anyway for all aspects of your gardening. You may require an electricity supply if you are going to have pumps or lighting, and the expense of connecting to your nearest outlet should be taken into consideration.

Take all these points into consideration before you build your pond and plan very carefully before selecting the final site. Remember that once the pond is built, it may require a lot of worry and expense to move it or remove it at a later date. However enthusiastic you may be about having a pond, do not rush into construction, only to find later that you have something which is "just not quite right !"

POND DESIGN

A pond can be as large or as small as you wish and can afford; its shape and complexity are limited only by your imagination. At little expense, a small hole in the ground and a liner can give you an attractive little pond suitable for a few plants and a couple of fish, while a great deal of work and plenty of money can give you a complicated system of different level ponds, streams, waterfalls, fountains and bog gardens.

Ornamental ponds can be loosely divided into two types: the formal, and the informal or natural. The formal pond, as its name suggests, is symmetrical in design (square, rectangular, or circular, for example) and is usually the central focal point of a formal garden. Such ponds became very popular in the estates of the European aristocracy in the 17th and 18th centuries. Some magnificent examples of such ponds are still to be seen today on many of these estates, which are now open to the public. Raised walls, fountains and statuettes are usual features of a formal pond.

The informal pond is usually made using some random shape (kidney shape is very popular) and designed to look like a natural feature of an informal landscape. Such ponds frequently feature a waterfall and a bog garden and perhaps a narrow stretch which may be crossed by an ornamental bridge or a series of stepping stones. Informal ponds have softer lines that can be made to blend into almost any corner of the garden.

Your decision regarding a formal or informal pond may be influenced by the existing garden. If the garden is

already symmetrically designed, then the choice must rest with a formal pond. If the garden is casually laid out, perhaps with a "nature reserve" or two, then an informal pond will be your choice. The two types of pond would look out of place in the wrong settings. Whether your pond

Dr. Axelrod's koi pond is concrete and surrounded by stones which are used for sitting. Being at the edge of the sea, many sea birds visit the pond and can eat the smaller koi and goldfish. Photo by Dr. Herbert R. Axelrod.

is to be formal and elegant, or informal and more natural in appearance, there are certain physical limitations which must be borne in mind before you start contruction.

A pond should preferably be as large as space and finance allows. In general, a

larger pond is much easier to maintain than a small pond. A pond can never be too big for fish, but it can be too small for them. If you only intend to build a very small pond, then it will perhaps be better to dispense with the idea of keeping fish and be content just with the plants. The minimum size for a fish

pond should be 2 meters (6.5 ft.) by 1.5 meters (5 ft.) with a capacity of about 900 liters (approx. 200 gallons). With such a small pond you will, of course, be limited to the number of fish and water plants you can keep, but it can be made practical and attractive. In smaller ponds,

A wooden bridge is used to cross this garden pond. This type of bridge affords the ability to view the fishes from above, which is essentially the way most garden fishes (koi, goldfish, etc.) are ment to be viewed. Photo by Dr. Herbert R. Axelrod.

This formal garden pond, surrounded by Italian marble, is quite an elaborate and expensive construction. Photo by Dr. Herbert R. Axelrod.

results of natural decay will be quickly diluted and dispersed by the sheer volume of water.

Another point to bear in mind is that, if a small pond is subjected to accidental pollution by insecticides, herbicides or other such chemicals, the results can be

Another view of the bridged pond. This is a view from the house. Anyone visiting the house must come over the bridge. Thus the bridge has the secondary function of being a security factor. Photo by Dr. Herbert R. Axelrod.

the water will be subjected to dramatic temperature changes, depending on the weather, and small bodies of water obviously tend to be more quickly polluted by falling leaves and other such hazards. Dead and decaying plants and animals in a small-capacity pond will cause the water to quickly become smelly and dirty, producing large amounts of gases which will soon kill off all life in the pond. In larger ponds, however, the

quickly disastrous; whereas, the water volume in a large pond will quickly dilute the pollutant to less dangerous levels.

FISH POPULATION

The number of fish which can be safely kept in a pond will depend on the volume of the water and, more importantly, the size of the water surface area. Regular gas exchange takes place at the water surface; the

A magnificent Japanese koi pond with igneous rocks which don't dissolve, crystal clear water and champion koi. Photo by Shoichi Suda.

respiratory waste product of the fish and other animals (carbon dioxide) is released into the atmosphere and its place is taken by atmospheric oxygen. All aquatic animals require an adequate supply of oxygen to remain healthy, so your numbers of fish will depend on the amount of oxygen which the water can absorb from the atmosphere (plus oxygen given off by plants).

A good rule of thumb is to allow 155 square centimeters of water surface area to each 2.5cm of a fish's body length, excluding the tail. This can also be expressed as approximately 24 sq. in. of surface area for each inch of fish. When making a calculation, we must allow for the size to which the fish are eventually expected to grow; for example, they may be only 7.5cm (3 in.) long when we put them in the pond, but they may grow to 30cm (12 in.) or more and require a correspondingly larger amount of oxygen. Additionally, they will produce greater amounts of carbon dioxide. As an example, say we have a pond which is 3 meters long and 2 meters wide (approx. 10 ft. x

Two photos showing a water spout which falls onto a large stone from which the water trickles into the pond without causing problems for small fishes and delicate plants. Photo from Fotoarchiv Sammer.

6.5 ft.). The water surface area will be approximately 60,000 sq cm (or 9360 sq. in.). If we divide these measurements by 155cm (or 24 in.), we will find we have approximately 390 units of water area, each of which will allow 2.5cm (1 in.) of fish. If all our fish are to grow to 30cm (12 in.), we can work out how many fish we can place in the pond. In the case of centimeters, we divide the 30 by 2.5 (giving 12, the same as the inches). The 390 units are divided by 12, giving 32. We can therefore keep 32 fish of a potential 30cm (12 in.) body length in this pond. Of course we could also keep 64 15cm (6 in.) fish or 128 7.5cm (3 in.) fish, or any combination, provided the total length of fish body does not exceed the rule of 2.5cm per 155 sq cm surface area, or 1 in. of fish per 24 sq. in. of surface area.

The water depth is another important factor; the above rule would be useless if the water was only a few centimeters in depth. There must also be volume to hold the dissolved oxygen and disperse the waste carbon dioxide. The minimum average depth of the pond should be 30cm (12 in.). This will allow for deeper and shallower areas. Some of the deeper areas should be not less than 50cm (20 in.) deep, preferably more; you cannot really go too deep (within reason), and it is perhaps best to aim to have some areas being 1 meter (39 in.) deep. This is especially important in areas which experience extremes of climate. Depth

will prevent the fish (and some delicate water plants) from freezing in the winter and overheating in the summer. During extremes of temperature, the fish will be able to congregate in the relatively stable temperature of the deepest parts. A pond which is, say, 3 meters long, 2 meters wide, and 1 meter deep is, however, better than one which is 3 meters long, one meter wide, and two meters deep. They both have a similar

You have to look closely, but a fish eagle is scooping up a fish which was swimming on the top of this small molded pond. This is a daily demonstration in Singapore at the public bird farm. Photo by Dr. Herbert R. Axelrod.

volume of water, but the first has twice the surface area, thus allowing for a greater number of fish and plants.

If you intend to breed fish in your pond, you should provide some very shallow areas around the margins. Goldfish like to spawn in shallow parts of the pond, and the depth need be no more than 10cm (4 in.). However, do not construct too great an area of shallow parts at the expense of the deeper areas. Depending on the size of the pond, the spawning areas can

extend all around, or be situated at one or both ends. Such shallow areas also provide ideal planting sites for marginal plants.

If, for reasons of space and/ or expense, you are able to construct only a very small pond, do not let this worry you unduly. As long as you have the time and enthusiasm, the little extra maintenance required by the smaller pond will be well worth the effort. Shallower

pools will require some means of heating in the winter to prevent them freezing over entirely. An aquarium or immersion heater will do the job, but it will be necessary to have an electrical outlet close at hand. Great care must be taken to prevent a buildup of leaves or dead vegetation. In the fall, when deciduous trees are shedding their leaves, it is best to place a protective net over the smaller pond; otherwise you will have to net the leaves out of the water every day.

OPTIONAL EXTRAS

There are a number of extras which you can use with your pond, both to improve the visual appeal and to help with its maintenance. Before building your pond, you should decide exactly what extras you desire and include them in your design, as it will be more difficult to make alterations later.

Fountains and waterfalls are not only attractive, but they help increase the area of water which is exposed to the atmosphere and thus improve the oxygen supply. The maintenance of ponds can be vastly improved by the inclusion of a filter, which will

A typical luxurious English formal water garden. Photo by Hugh Nicholas.

Several ponds can be connected during the spring to allow the fishes to spawn. Once they have spawned, the adults are moved to one pond and the fry are allowed to grow in the other pond.

remove suspended solids from the water. There are many kinds of pond filters on the market, ranging from simple gravity sand or gravel filters to expensive and elaborate units which will keep the pond water crystal clear at all times. Whatever kind of filter you use, it will require regular maintenance and changing of the filter medium. Of course, a pump or pumps and the necessary electricity supply will be required to operate these additions, and it may be convenient to conceal the housing of these appliances in your design. You may want to conceal the pipes running from the pump to the waterfall or fountain outlet, but be sure not to make these items too inaccessible in case you need to get at them for maintenance.

Lighting as a night feature also has its merits, particularly with regard to the patio pond. You may prefer to have spotlights or colored underwater lighting. Again,

Garden ponds require excellent filtration, especially when keeping any quantity of goldfish or koi. Photo courtesy of Eheim.

provisions for the installation of lighting equipment should be made at the design stage, ensuring that each part of it will be easily accessible for maintenance.

Always remember that electricity and water are a dangerous mixture and, unless you are competent in such matters, all electrical installations should be installed by an experienced electrician. Although improvisation is a virtue for the pond builder, on no account should you skimp on electrical fittings; only buy appliances which are designed and manufactured for such use. Some local authorities also have stringent regulations governing the installation and use of outdoor electrical fittings, so ensure that you abide by the rules rather than risk accident or prosecution.

This concrete pond with its statues, which also serve as sources of fresh water, is planted with water lilies. Photo by V. Capaldi.

CONSTRUCTING A POND

Having decided on whether to have a formal or informal pond and where it is to be sited, the type of construction must be considered. There are several ways of constructing a pond and these will be discussed individually.

PRE-FABRICATED POOLS

Perhaps the easiest of all pools to install are the commercially obtainable pre-fabricated designs. Most of these are in the small- to medium-sized range and are constructed on molds from PVC or fiber glass. Such pools are rigid in construction, may be available in formal or informal design, and usually have varying depths, with shallow areas for marginal plants, etc. All that is required to install such a pool is an excavation in the ground, roughly the size of the pool, taking care to remove any sharp rocks from between the lining and the surrounding soil, as the weight of the water could damage the pool and cause leakage. Some soft sand should be placed in the base of the excavation and the pool lowered into position. You may have to use a straight edge and a spirit level to get the top edges of the pond level. If one end is too deep, you can adjust the level by adding or removing sand. When the pool has been set firmly in the ground, the space between the wall of the pool and the excavation should be filled with soft sand or sieved earth. The rim of the pond may be disguised with flat rocks or paving.

The two photos above show Dr. Axelrod's pond by the sea. The pond is readied for planting the decorative edge plants early in the spring. Photos by Dr. Axelrod.

LINED POOLS

Perhaps not quite so easy to construct as the pre-fabricated pool, the lined pool can still usually be installed quickly and with the minimum of difficulty; in recent years, this has become probably the most popular type of pool for the home garden. The basis of the pool is the waterproof flexible pool liner which is placed in an excavation and filled with water. The weight of the water pulls the liner into the shape of the excavation; therefore, a pond of almost any shape can be constructed. Such a pool is probably the cheapest of all to construct but usually has a

In the photo above, Dr. Herbert R. Axelrod, probably the most prolific and popular of writers on the subject of garden ponds and koi, sets his automatic overflow filter. Below: Children visiting Dr. Axelrod's home are warned about falling into the pond. The underwater edges around the pond are actually stairs so anyone falling into the water (including stray dogs), can easily get out.

excavation and will tolerate the pressures of ice and frost. If using builder's polyethylene sheeting, it is inexpensive enough to install a double, or even triple, layer as added insurance against accidental damage.

To construct a lined pool, first of all excavate the soil to the required size, shape, and depth. To be at its most natural looking, such a pool is best constructed on level ground; however, a pool may be constructed on slightly sloping ground by using some of the contents from the excavation to build up the lower level. With a lined pond, all edges must be at an even level all the way round, otherwise you will be left with an ugly and unnatural view of part of the liner after the pond has been filled. A minimum depth of 76cm (30 in.) is recommended at the center of the pool, and this can gently slope towards ground level at one end. At the other end you can excavate a shelf for marginal plants. Ideas for the inner contours of the pond often arise during construction, and some very interesting combinations of depths are possible. Remove all sharp projections, such as rocks and roots, and rake over the whole area to remove loose stones, etc. Imperfections may be filled with soft sand or sieved soil.

The size of the liner should be that of the pond's surface dimensions plus twice the maximum depth, plus one meter each way. Thus, as an example, if you have a pond 3 meters (10 ft.) long, 2 meters (6.5 ft.) wide, and 1 meter (3.25 ft.) (maximum) deep, your liner should be 6 meters

limited life. Punctures in the liner are almost bound to occur eventually, and they are extremely difficult to repair. Various materials may be used as a liner, ranging from heavy gauge builder's polyethylene sheeting (of the type used to damp-proof concrete floors, etc.) to PVC or butyl rubber. Some manufacturers now produce very durable liners, often reinforced with nylon, specially for pool construction. Such liners have exceptional strength and are elastic enough to withstand all but the sharpest of imperfections in the

THE CONSTRUCTION OF THE LINED POND

The construction of a lined pond is not difficult if you follow these simple illustrated steps. If you have ANY problems, discuss them with the person from whom you bought the liner. Do NOT accept any liner without a guarantee that it won't leak and has no holes, even though fixing small holes are tears is not much of a problem before the liner is installed. The steps to follow are as follows:

1. Using a garden hose or heavy rope, lay out the design of the pond on the turf or grass and dig down about 4 inches to make a shelf upon which you will eventually lay stones to hold the plastic liner in position.

2. Excavate around the form you have designed and make a few terraces to that animals or children can escape easily if they fall into the pond. The top shelf must be as level as possible since it will hold flat stones.

3. Use a leveling device to ascertain the levelness of the shelf. This is a critical move as you want even pressure to hold the plastic liner in place.

4. After completing the first shelf, you can now devote your attention to the second shelf. This is, in reality, a step for people and animals should they fall in. It also serves as a shelf for potted plants which can be lowered as they grow in height since the amount of light available at lower depths is not always suitable to lighting-loving plants.

5. Loose sand is put into place against the inside walls to smooth out any holes or spots which might help in the puncturing of the liner.

6. The excavation work is completed when the pond is laid out with the shelving in place and the shelves being leveled.

Photos courtesy of Stapely Water Gardens.

THE CONSTRUCTION OF THE LINED POND

Continued from page 16.

7. The liner is carefully and loosely laid over the excavation as neatly as possible. A small amount of water is added slowly to anchor the plastic against the bottom.

8. When you are sure that the liner will be uniformly covering the pond when filled with water, you can slowly begin to fill the pond.

9. When the pond is filled to the level of the top shelf, the plastic is rolled back to be completely covered by stones. No plastic liner should extend above the stones.

10. The stones are now put into place to hold the liner. This is the most difficult step because you have to have some experience with cutting the stones so they will closely fit to one another.

11. The stones should be cemented together and the water allowed to age for a week or two. During this interlude you can be ordering statues, filters, water lilies and other aquatic and semi-aquatic vegetation.

12. When the pond is all finished, bring up a chair, sit down and enjoy your handicraft. It is estimated that there are 35 man-hours of toil involved in this project.

Photos courtesy of Stapely Water Gardens.

Two views of a lovely liner pond made by Roger Knox. Photos by Peter Farley.

long and 5 meters wide (approx. 20 x 16 ft.). It is better to have the liner a little too large than a little too small; you can always cut off the excess, but you cannot add to it! The liner (which is preferably of a dark color) is placed over the whole of the excavation and allowed to fall partly into it. Do not attempt to lay the liner into the contours. The edges of the liner should be weighted all around with heavy objects (bricks, rocks, etc). Water can then be slowly run into the liner which, as the weight increases, will be molded into the contours of the excavation. Keep a close watch as the liner is being filled and, should any undue strain occur at any of the weights, remove them and allow the liner to pull itself gently out of strain.

When the pool is filled, about 60cm (2 ft.) of lining should be left all around the edges and the excess can be trimmed off. The edges are disguised under flat rocks or paving. If the pond is on a lawn, the turf may be cut and folded back, the edges of the liner laid under it and the turf replaced. With a lined pool, great care should be taken not to damage the liner during construction or afterwards. Be careful with sharp instruments such as the garden fork or rake. Never build the pool too close to trees or shrubs with large root systems which could pierce the liner. Do not allow children or animals to play in the pool; the author has seen a large lined pool destroyed in seconds by the powerful claws of a playful German Shepherd Dog! With lined pools, it is best to place all of the aquatic

plants in pots, thus keeping disturbance of the liner to a minimum.

THE CONCRETE POOL

Until the comparatively recent advent of pre-fabricated and lined pools, the concrete pool was the most popular type for those requiring a fairly permanent structure. Carefully planned and constructed, a concrete pool is the most durable and lasting

type of pool and has the added advantage of the ease in which additional features, such as waterfalls, can be included in the overall design. A concrete pool is perhaps the most expensive and time-consuming type to construct, but it will be well worth the effort as, with a few weekends of work, the enthusiast can make a landscaped pond which will not only provide an ideal home for his fish and

Massive pools can be constructed of cement with large stones imbedded into the cement. This Japanese garden is fed by rainwater and the water drains all empty into the koi pond. Photo courtesy of Takeshi Yokoyama.

An above-the ground water garden is possible even on a minimum amount of available land in the middle of the city. Photo courtesy of V. Capaldi.

plants, but will become an integral feature of the garden and an object of many years' pleasure. The traditional method of preparing a concrete pool was to make an excavation, pack the base with suitable fill, and line the interior with a 10cm (4 in.) layer of concrete. This method is still used by some home builders. A newer method is to have a specialist contractor pressure spray the concrete, thus forming a watertight shell.

Unless built very carefully and with a great deal of forethought, a concrete pool is likely to leak. As an insurance against leakage, a very permanent pool can be constructed using a waterproof liner and concrete. There are several methods which may be used in the construction of a concrete pond; a successful method tried and tested by the author will now be explained.

First of all, it must be decided whether the pool is to be formal or informal in design, and this may well depend on the existing layout of the garden. A plan of the pond should then be drawn up. Siting, size, type of subsoil, and drainage should be considered before construction begins. A formal pond is usually somewhat easier to construct because its sides are straight and simpler to cast. Mark out the shape of the intended pool (with pegs and string or with sprinkled sand) and excavate to the required contours and depth. The excavation should be about 30cm (12 in.) deeper than the eventual water depth. Allow for the walls to slope slightly outwards so that

Contrasting with the small pond on the facing page where land was at a premium, we have a garden pond which was constructed in the countryside, with ample land to satisfy every need. Photo by Hugh Nicholas.

if the pond should freeze over in the winter, the ice will push upwards rather than forcing squarely against the walls of the pond.

A drain will be of considerable assistance when the time arrives to empty the pond for cleaning, and this should be incorporated at this stage. A 5-cm (2-in.) diameter pipe should be laid, with its inlet at the deepest part of the pool. This should run to an existing drain, a ditch, or a dry well (which will, of course, have to be at a lower level than the pond). If the installation of a drain will pose too many difficulties (as when the ground

is too level to allow a reasonable drainage slope), it will perhaps be best to dispense with the drain and to rely on a pump for emptying the pond. If a dry well is to be used, this should be deeper and three times the volume of the pond and filled with large stones and rubble, so that the entire contents of the pond can be drained away at once. Alternatively, a smaller dry well can be constructed and the bulk of the water removed by siphon or pump and when the pond is almost empty, the remainder can be drained into it. The best method of releasing the water from the pond is by

means of a gate valve, situated in the drain pipe in a small concealed chamber outside the pond. During construction, ensure that the drain inlet is protected to prevent rubble or concrete from gaining access and blocking it.

Firmly pack a 15cm-(6-in.) layer of suitable fill all over the base of the excavation and cover this with a 5cm-(2-in.) layer of pea gravel or coarse sand. A double layer of builder's polyethylene sheeting is then laid in the excavation to provide a waterproof layer (a small hole will have to be made in this for the drain inlet).

Garden ponds don't have to be large to be beautiful. This small pond measures 3 x 5 meters (10 x 15 feet) and is decorated with water lilies in the pond and many types of border plants. The danger with a pond like this is that pets or people can easily fall into the pond. But this pond is very shallow, for safety reasons.

The concrete, consisting of one part cement to two parts sharp sand and four parts gravel,is mixed with water to a smooth, but not too runny, consistency and the base areas are laid first to a thickness of about 10cm (4 in.) over the waterproof sheeting, taking care not to damage this in the process. As reinforcement, 5cm (2 in.) galvanized wire netting can be laid in the center of the

boards. They are made into something like a box with no base and no lid and of a size which will leave about 15 cm (6 in.) of space between the boarding and the excavated walls. The reinforcing wire (if used) is placed in position and the concrete is fed into the space between the boards and the waterproofing sheet. It is then compacted by beating the board at intervals with a

should be covered with a waterproof sheet to prevent the rain from pockmarking the surface.

An alternative method of building up the walls of the pond is to use bricks or concrete blocks instead of shuttered concrete. In such cases, the concrete base of the pond should be thicker (say 30 cm - 12 in.) around its edges to give a supporting foundation.

A magnificent garden pond in Japan featuring a stone bridge, water lilies and irises.

concrete, ensuring that it does not come through the surface at any point. The concrete should be tapped down with a straight- edge and smoothed over with a trowel to give a reasonably flat surface. When the base is beginning to harden, a properly sized groove for the walls should be scored in its surface for about 15 cm (6 in.) around its edges. The walls of the pond may be cast by using wooden shuttering

hammer. The shuttering should be left for at least 72 hours for the concrete to set before it is carefully removed. During very hot, dry weather, it is advisable to cover setting concrete with damp burlap and finely spray it with water at regular intervals; this will prevent the concrete from drying out too quickly and cracking. If there is a likelihood of rain during the setting time, the concrete

The bricks are built up in front of the waterproofing sheet and can slope slightly outwards. A good quality mortar is used to cement the bricks together and more mortar can be packed behind the bricks for added strength. An even stronger construction can be made by having a double wall with the waterproofing sheet in between. After building the wall, the interior surface is faced with a double layer of cement rendering. Mortar is applied to the surfaces with a plastering trowel and, when it is nearly set, it is scored to give a key for the final coat. The final coat can be applied the next day and, when this is nearly set, it may be smoothed over with a wet sponge. For a smoother finish, the set surface can be painted over with a wet mixture of one part cement to one part soft sand.

As cement contains free lime, this will be released through the surface of the concrete and appear as a whitish deposit. Excess lime must be removed before any plants or fish are installed in the pond or the high alkalinity will pose a hazard. When the concrete has set, the pond should be filled with water and left for 48 hours. Then drain or pump the water away and scrub the lime deposits off the concrete surface and swill clean. The process should be repeated about three times or until all traces of the lime have disappeared.

If you do not have a waterproof liner under your concrete, or if you want to further seal the concrete surface to prevent lime release, you can apply a coat of commercial pond-sealer to the surface. Several brands of sealer are manufactured especially for this purpose and all of these not only render the pond watertight, but also neutralize the effect of the lime in the cement which could be harmful to both fish and plants. The primer and sealer should be applied following the manufacturer's instructions and allowed to dry. Fill the pool once more with water, leave for 48 hours, drain, scrub and rinse before preparation for stocking.

THE RAISED POOL

The raised pool is constructed in much the same manner as the concrete pool, except that a wall extends above the ground level. The waterproof sheet can be brought up in between the double wall, and the inside of the wall should be rendered as for the normal pond. Raised pools are more likely to be formal in shape, although they are useful in cases of sloping land for all types of pools.

If you only have a small space, even a balcony, there are sink and tub garden ponds which can be as much fun as a full-sized garden pond. Photo courtesy of Van Ness Water Gardens.

Huge, pre-fabricated swimming pools are easily converted to garden ponds. Such pools often have to be surrounded by fencing to protect against pets and people from falling in. Your local swimming pool contractor can usually supply you with a large pre-fabricated pond.

THE POND SURROUNDINGS

The pond surroundings are just as important as the pond itself; it would be pointless having a beautifully designed and planted pool if it was surrounded with dirty, litter strewn, muddy areas. The pond should have a fairly solid path around at least half of its sides so that one has comfortable access for viewing. Brick, concrete slab or paving, often used to match existing paths, are all ideal. The other sides of the pond can consist of rock gardens, plain flower beds or expanses of lawn. A raised area towards what one would normally consider to be the rear of the pond (i.e. the side of the pond farthest away from the direction in which one mainly views it) certainly improves the perspective and naturalness of a pond. It is a good idea to place the earth from the initial excavation of the pool in a position where it can easily be used to create such a feature.

MOVING WATER FEATURES

A waterfall, fountain or stream will add to the overall effect of your water garden. There are both advantages and disadvantages of having a moving water feature but the former outweigh the latter. Advantages are that the feature will provide sound as well as movement to improve the aesthetics of the design; moving water also increases the exchange of gases, provides extra oxygen from the air and helps keep the water fresher. It prevents debris and dust from settling and forming a surface scum and it inhibits the growth of floating algae, the cause of the so-called "green water". If used in conjunction with a filter (usually only necessary when large numbers of "messy" fish such are Koi are kept), a waterfall will further help to keep the water clear of suspended solids.

Disadvantages are fewer and can usually be overcome; fountains and waterfalls will reduce or increase the overall temperature of the water depending on the season. If the pond is of sufficient volume, this should be of no consequence in the summer. However, in hard winters, a waterfall or fountain should preferably be switched off so that the deeper part of the pond can retain its life-supporting warmer temperatures. Some aquatic plants (particularly water lilies) will not perform well if continually doused with falling water; the blooms will just close up and submerge. However, it is possible to install a fountain or a waterfall away from the main planted area.

Formal ponds are more likely to have a fountain (which is really an unnatural phenomenon unless you take geysers into account), while informal ponds are best equipped with a waterfall and/or a stream. The ambitious water gardener, particularly one with the necessary sloping land, can construct two or more ponds at different levels with streams and waterfalls running from

Architect Albert Spalding Benoist, who specializes in garden ponds among other things, sketched his dream pond.

Water Hyacinths clog the top of this small pond. The solid plant cover protects the small pond from algae blooms and fish-eating birds.

A very informal garden pond where the pond is part of the total garden and must fit in rather unobtrusively.

Left: A side view of the informal water garden shown above right.

Below: Algae are a very serious water garden problem. The final resolution of the problem is the construction of a gazebo over the top of the garden to keep the light out.

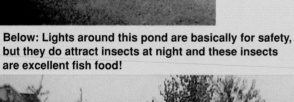

Below: Lights around this pond are basically for safety, but they do attract insects at night and these insects are excellent fish food!

the highest to the lowest levels. Alternatively, the owner of a single small pond may like to use the excavated earth to form a basis for a small waterfall.

Artificial waterfalls and fountains are usually operated by an electrically driven pump of which there are two basic kinds available—submersible and surface. The former is easier to install and usually less expensive; it operates totally under water and the whole assembly is contained in a single unit. The submersible pump is much preferable to the surface pump; it is soundless and, as it is concealed below the water surface, is less likely to suffer priming problems and does not require additional protective and concealing housing, as a surface pump would. Submersible pumps may be used for a fountain or a waterfall, the fountain head and waterfall pipe attachments being interchangeable. These pumps are obtainable in various sizes, depending on the volume of water to be moved; so there is a size suitable for most ponds. The pump should be situated firmly on raised bricks or blocks (to keep the inlet strainer free of substrate mulm) in a deeper part of the lowest pond. In the case of a fountain, the fountain head pipe should reach just to the surface of the water or be attached to the fountain superstructure if used.

An electrical supply to the area will be necessary to operate the pump. Pumps themselves are fitted with safety measures controlled by government specifications in most countries. Ensure that you buy a pump covered by these safety regulations and do not try to improvise. To prevent accidents, great care should be taken in the installation of the supply. A heavy duty cable should be used and this should preferably be concealed and run through a protective conduit. The power point should be placed in a

Large garden ponds usually have electrically driven pumps and filters, lights for paths and in the water, too. When initially planning the pond, keep electrical needs in mind. Photo by Hugh Nicholas.

concealed weatherproof box, placed at a point well above the water surface where it cannot be affected by flooding. However adept you are at do-it-yourself procedures, you are well advised to obtain the services of a qualified electrician to install your outdoor supply.

THE WATERFALL

If you are installing a waterfall, a (usually flexible) pipe is attached to the pump outlet and taken to the point where the waterfall is to start. The pipe can be buried in a trench running up the side of the waterfall area. The pipe outlet can be concealed under one or two rocks cemented together to make the emergence of the water look more natural. Alternatively, the outlet can be under the water in a small pool at the head of the waterfall.

Careful planning is required with waterfall and stream construction. The surfaces over which the water will run must be just as watertight as the pond itself, otherwise you will have to be continually topping off. Also, a waterfall will increase the amount of water lost through evaporation so, at times of drought or water shortage, it will be best to leave the waterfall pump switched off. If you live in an area where water supply poses no problems, you could install a concealed cistern with a ballcock in the lowest pool and then you will never have any topping off problems.

To build a waterfall and stream, you must first ensure that the base of the areas over which the water is to run is solid and stable, especially if you are using excavated earth

A water garden ablaze with flowers doesn't leave much room for people who want to look into the pond. Initially the pond had huge rocks upon which people could sit, gaze and ponder. Photo by Michael Gilroy.

There are many kinds of water fountains available from dealers. Fountains or sprays are necessary for aerating the pond.

which are cemented together but with small holes left, through which water can seep into the growing medium contained in the basin, keeping it moist. By regulating the amount of moisture available to the various growing areas, you can create additional ideal situations for moisture-loving plants such as ferns or mosses, as well as the more conventional bog plants.

THE FOUNTAIN

Various kinds of pump-driven fountains are available from dealers. These include straightforward types which push the water into the air and various spouting ornaments which will force the water in any direction you require. The latter include such figures as dolphins, seals, frogs, lions' heads, humans, mermaids, etc. The fountain may be mounted in the center of the pool or on a wall at the rear of the pool. Care should be taken to ensure that all of the water from fountains and spouts is directed back into the pool and not elsewhere.

A particularly attractive kind of central fountain and cascade can be made by building up a pyramidal tower of natural rocks with a supply pipe through the middle. The fountain head can then be mounted on top of the tower and the water will cascade down the rocks. A bird bath can be mounted on top of the pyramid so that the falling water is spread evenly.

POOL FILTERS

The pondkeepers of today are tending to use filtration systems more than ever to

from the pond. It is advisable to include solid material (rocks, brick rubble, etc.) in the construction of the mound and ensure that it is thoroughly packed and compounded into position. Natural rocks can be used to create the waterfall and stream areas. These are let into the mound in the desired position and cemented together. Waterproof sheeting is placed in the bases of the water channels and this is covered with further rocks and concrete. By skillful use of a dry paint brush, you can tap and sculpt the concrete to match up with the rocks you are using, thus helping to disguise the joints. After a few months weathering you will then barely be able to distinguish what is concrete and what is natural rock. For best effect, a waterfall should have one or two areas where

the water runs over a flat, level lip, thus spreading the water into a wide contour. This can be achieved by cementing a flat rock in front of a small pool along the water course. Several smaller falls are often more pleasing than a single big drop. After the concrete and cement have set, you can switch on the pump and give the waterfall a trial run, looking carefully for any points where the water overflows and escapes into areas where it cannot return to the pond. If water is escaping at any point, turn off the waterfall and repair the escape areas with fillets of cement and/or more rocks.

Bog areas can be incorporated along the edges of the streams and waterfalls by building waterproof basins adjacent to the water course. The basins are separated from the water course by rocks improve the quality of the water in their ponds. While filtration is not strictly essential in the well-balanced ornamental pond, it will certainly do no harm to install a simple system, especially if you plan to have a waterfall anyway. A filtration system will remove floating and suspended solids from the water and help keep the water crystal clear. If you desire to keep more than the prescribed number of fishes in a pond for breeding purposes, then it is advisable to have a system of filtration. A filter system has to be maintained at regular intervals, but the time spent in doing this is compensated for by the fact that the pond itself will require less maintenance. It is possible to purchase ready-made filtration systems of various kinds, which can be installed directly into your waterfall circulation system. They range from simple gravity-fed containers to complex systems through which the water is forced by a powerful pump. The average home pondkeeper is not likely to require a very powerful filter. Tropical fish specialty stores and pet shops that sell tropical fish are good sources of supply and information about pond filters.

POOL LIGHTING
   Today, sophisticated lighting equipment enables us to increase the attractiveness of our ponds at night by illuminating the water, cascades and fountains, as well as surrounding areas. Such illumination is of particular merit when used in areas where outdoor entertaining is prevalent. An illuminated pond next to the

There is nothing more peaceful, beautiful and effective for a water pond's success than the gentle waterfall. Photo by M. Gilroy.

patio is indeed romantic. There are lamps available which can be lit from above or below water. Waterproof lamps can be floated on the water surface or completely submerged, while external floodlighting equipment can be concealed in strategic positions around the pool. Such lamps are mounted on spikes which can be pushed into the soil and the direction of the light then adjusted to angles which will illuminate poolside trees and shrubs. Other lamps may be mounted overhead on walls or poles; there is no limit to the amount of ideas one can come up with.

Various colored lamps are available, but these should be used with discretion if one is to avoid a circus effect. The most aesthetic effects can be produced by using white light which will accentuate the natural colors of the plants.

However, a few lights of other colors—used carefully—can add to the overall effect. Fountains and waterfalls are particularly attractive when illuminated. The light catches the iridescent sheen of the spray and thus greatly increases the enjoyment one may gain from a water feature at night.

Needless to say, and as already mentioned for electrical pumps, strict safety procedures must be followed when wiring the power to illuminations. Only the type of equipment which is specially manufactured for the job in question should be used.

Water is sprayed over the rock in the background and gently drips into the garden pond. Eventually the rocks get covered with moss. Photo by John Marks.

AQUATIC PLANTS

No garden pond is complete without its aquatic plants. Not only do they make the pond more natural and add to its aesthetic appeal, the plants themselves are almost essential to the ecological balance of the pond and its inhabitants. If we look at various natural ponds, we will see that they may be populated with various kinds of plants ranging from simple unicellular species to semi-aquatic trees in which the roots are continually immersed in water. In the garden pond we are mainly concerned with those species which add to its appeal and improve its balance, as well as to provide refuge, shade and spawning sites for the fish.

BASIC BOTANY

The successful aquaculturist, like the adept gardener, must have at least a little basic knowledge of botany in order to ensure that his aquatic plants can thrive. Just as zoology is the scientific study of members of the animal kingdom, so botany encompasses research into every aspect of the realm of plants— ranging from the simplest microscopic unicellular forms to the largest of all life forms, the trees. Pure botany can be an extremely complicated subject, but do not let this alarm you; in your pond, you will only be concerned with the basics. As in zoology, there are many sub-disciplines in botany, some of which may assist us in our aquacultural interests. The main branches which interest us are taxonomy (the study of classifying and naming plants and animals), physiology (the examination of the functions of their internal structure), and ecology (the science of the interactions of all living things with each other and their natural environment).

TYPES OF WATER PLANTS

The types of water plants which we can grow in and around our pond include:

Submerged plants which root into the substrate and stay wholly submerged, with the exception of the flowers and related foliage in some species.

Floating foliage plants which root into the substrate and have leaves and flowers which float horizontally on the water surface.

Floating plants the major parts of which float on the water surface; may be rootless, have hanging roots, or roots which reach down to the substrate.

Marginal plants in which only the root stock is

Sometimes a pond becomes choked with water plants. These healthy plants were simply harvested and put to good use elsewhere. Photo by Lothar Wischnath.

submerged, the remainder being above the water surface.

Bog plants which thrive in damp conditions but with no part thoroughly submerged (except in flood conditions).

This method of classifying our plants is not strictly botanical; indeed, there will be some plants which are closely related botanically but may fall into separate groups. The purpose of this kind of classification is that one can choose plants to suit each different area of the pond and thus create an aesthetic balance. There are many hundreds of different species, hybrids, and varieties which can be used in and around the ornamental pond, and new types are continually being brought to the attention of the aquaculturist. In a volume of this size, it would be impossible to describe more than a cross-section of the types available, so the author has chosen to select a number of the more common and well known species. Most of those described are inexpensive, easy to cultivate, and serve the purposes of decoration, oxygenation, and recycling of waste materials, as well as providing shade, refuge and spawning sites for the fishes.

Note: In this chapter we'll consider only submerged plants. Floating foliage plants and floating and marginal plants will be discussed in the two following chapters. Plants are usually obtained from a dealer (aquatic nurseryman) or from a fellow aquaculturist or pondkeeper (most species grow so well that they have to be thinned out at regular intervals; this is the time to scrounge your cuttings and clumps!). When purchasing plants, only select stock which appears healthy and has good signs of vigorous growth. Avoid plants with signs of decay on the leaves, stems or rootstocks.

PLANTING AND CULTIVATION

Most kinds of plants used in and around the ornamental pond are best planted or transplanted in the spring or early summer, before the vegetative growth is too far advanced to be checked. At this time, the increasing amount of daylight and warmer temperatures will encourage quick root development so that the plants quickly become established in their new positions. However, submerged plants and floating plants of the type which possess no roots or hardly any roots can be moved at any time during the growing season.

During the summer months, in addition to controlling any pests or diseases which attack water plants, a certain amount of pruning may be required in order to keep vigorous plants under control, especially in smaller ponds where certain species can proliferate at the expense of others. Submerged plants which grow to such an extent that they overcrowd the pond can be removed by dragging them out in large clumps, either by hand or with a rake. All waste plant material can be used on the compost heap. Decaying leaves and spent flower heads should be removed. Floating leaves and surface scum can be removed with a large long-handled net.

In the fall, most of the aquatic plants will die down and this, in addition to the leaves of deciduous trees which are blown into the pond, will soon foul the water unless they are removed at regular intervals before they

Anubias lanceolata.

sink. One way of preventing leaves from getting into the pool is to lay a plastic or wire mesh over a frame covering the pool at this time of the year.

SUBMERGED PLANTS

Anubias lanceolata

Anubias is a small genus of West African aquatic or semi-aquatic plants. They have creeping horizontal rhizomes and arum- like flowers. All of the species do best in soft water, and they are not suitable for areas likely to be affected by frost. The flowers and leaves will partly emerge through the water. *A. lanceolata* is one of the better known species, with long, dark-green, lanceolate leaves and green, fleshy flower

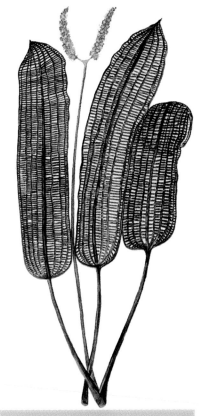

Aponogeton fenestralis, the Madagascar Lace Plant.

spathes. It may be propagated by root division.

Aponogeton

This is a large genus of aquatic plants from Asia, Africa, (particularly Madagascar) and Australia. All species require slightly acid water and warmer

temperatures, which should not fall below 60°F, even in the winter. Most of the species are tuberously rooted and are best suited to subtropical or tropical areas, but they can be cultivated successfully in aquaria and indoor ponds. Interesting species include *A. fenestralis* from Madagascar, which has oblong, perforated leaves up to 20cm (8 in.) in length. The perforations, or windows, gives them a lace-like appearance. *A. crispus*, from Sri Lanka, has long, narrow, bright green leaves up

Callitriche palustris.

to 30cm (12 in.) in length. The Australian *A. elongatus* has similar but more wavy edged leaves. All *Aponogeton* species bear spikes of whitish, pinkish or yellowish flowers above the water surface.

Callitriche hermaphroditica

C. hermaphroditica (Water Starwort) from Europe is a hardy aquatic and a good oxygenator for the outdoor pool. The long, thin, branching stems come to the surface in the summer months and form

rosettes of small leaves. A fast-growing plant with very small flowers, it may be propagated by division. Other related species with similar requirements include *C. hamsulata*, *C. palustris*, and *C. stagnalis*.

Ceratophyllum demersum

This species (also called Hornwort) and the closely related *C. submersum*, are very popular aquatic plants which can be used in temperate ponds and cold-water aquaria, where they are favored by spawning goldfish. The leaves are fine and feathery and the stalks may grow as long as 150cm (5 ft.)

Ceratophyllum demersum.

in water with a suitable depth. It is a totally submersed plant which actually flowers below the water surface. It may be propagated by taking cuttings or clumps, weighting them and planting them in a fairly dense clay-containing substrate. It is rather invasive and will require regular thinning out. However, it dies back in the winter, but dormant buds sink to the bottom of the pond and begin growing in the following spring. *C. submersum*, the spineless hornwort, with its greener and less turgid leaves, is a more delicate species

Nitella gracilis.

which may be cultivated in frost-free areas.

Chara (Nitella)

This genus, also called Stonewort, contains a number of hardy species suitable for the garden pond. The stems grow to about 20cm (8 in.) in length and they are furnished with whorls of leaves about 2.5cm (1 in.) in length. The stems are bristly and rough to the touch. *Charas* are able to extract lime from the water but they are not particularly good oxgenators. However, they are rapid growing and

provide shelter for the aquatic life in the pond. Species available include *C. aspera*, *C. globularis* and *C. gracilis*.

Crassula recurva

This is a creeping plant from Australia which will grow equally well under shallow water or at the pond's margins. The tiny, succulent leaves are only 4mm (1/7 in.) long and diminutive white flowers appear in the summer. It is a fairly hardy plant which may be propagated by division.

Crassula recurva.

Cryptocoryne

The genus *Cryptocoryne* contains a number of species very popular with aquarists. They are not very hardy and only suited to warmer areas or indoor pools where the temperature barely drops below 68°F Most are slow growing and require slightly acid conditions, achieved by

adding peat to the growing medium. The leaves of most species are lanceolate and come in various shades of green. In warm, light conditions, arum-shaped flowers are produced. The plants may be propagated by division. Some of the better known species include *C. affinis*, *C. becketti*, *C. ciliata*, *C. lutea*, *C. wendti* and *C. willisi.*

Egeria densa

Sometimes erroneously referred to as *Elodea* (another genus), this tropical South American species is an excellent oxygenator for pools in the warmer areas. It is reasonably hardy but cannot tolerate frosty conditions. Under favorable conditions, the stems, with their dense whorls of dark-green narrow leaves may reach two meters (6 ft.) or more in length. The small, white, three-petaled flowers are produced just

Cryptocoryne ciliata.

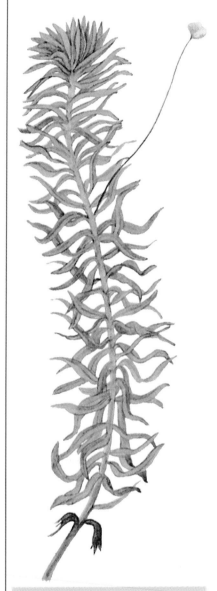

Egeria densa.

above the water surface, where they are pollinated by flying insects. It is readily propagated by inserting weighted cuttings into the substrate.

Elatine

This genus, also known as Waterwort, consists of small, many-branched, creeping aquatics. They have fragile, bright green, oval leaves and will grow throughout the year in favorable climates. The flowers are insignificant. Species hardy in temperate areas include *E. americana*, *E. hydropiper*, *E. hexandra*, and *E. macropoda*.

Eleocharis acicularis

This widespread species (also known as Hair Grass) is found in Europe, Asia and North America. It is hardy in all but the most severe of winters and will grow near to the pond margins where it forms tufts of

Eleocharis acicularis.

rush-like leaves up to 35cm (14 in.) in length. It produces small spikelets of flowers in late summer and fall. It may be propagated by division of the tuberous roots. The related *E. dulcis* is interesting on account of its edible crunchy white tubers, which are given the name of Chinese water chestnuts (often featured in Chinese menus). This is a tropical species which can only be cultivated in warmer climes.

Elodea canadensis

Also known as Canadian Pondweed, this is probably the most commonly used of all submerged plants in the ornamental pond and is ideal for the partially shaded site. It grows in long strands with small, rounded, dark green leaves growing in whorls along their length. It is usually purchased in bunches of stem cuttings and these should be weighted and buried a few centimeters in the substrate, where they will soon take root.

Elodea canadensis.

Fontinalis antipyretica.

Lobelia dortmanna.

The very small, pink, floating flowers are borne on thread-like stalks up to 15cm (6in.) in length. Under ideal conditions, *Elodea* grows very quickly and, if it is not regularly thinned out, it can take over the whole pond to the detriment of other species. Goldfish will graze on the leaves of this plant and help keep it in check. Other *Elodea* species include *E. nuttali* and *E. longivaginata*, which require milder conditions.

Fontinalis antipyretica

Also known as Water Moss, this plant is found in Europe, Asia and North America. This hardy species gets its specific name *antipyretica* from the fact that it was formerly used in Scandinavia to insulate the space between the fireplace and walls of houses, thus excluding air and preventing fire. In the wild, the plant is usually found in running water, where it attaches itself by its roots to rocks and stones. If collected in the wild, the anchor should preferably be taken with it; otherwise stem cuttings may be propagated by carefully tying them (with thread) to stones and immersing them in the water. The dark green, narrow leaves are densely packed along the branching stems.

Lobelia dortmanna

This hardy evergreen plant, known as Water Lobelia, is found in Europe and North America. It prefers relatively deep, clear, slightly acid water. It has tufts of stiff dark-green leaves about 10cm (4 in.) in length. In early summer it bears small, bell-shaped, white-banded, light-blue flowers above the water

surface. It may be propagated by division of the offshoots.

Myriophyllum

This genus of plants is highly valued by aquarists. Most species are attractive in appearance, are excellent oxygenators, and provide ideal spawning sites for many fish species. They are easily propagated by breaking off cuttings and simply inserting them in the substrate. The fine, feathery leaves are arranged in whorls along the stems. Hardy species suitable for outdoor temperate areas include *M. heterophyllum*, *M. spicatum*, and *M. verticillatum*.

Myriophyllum spicatum.

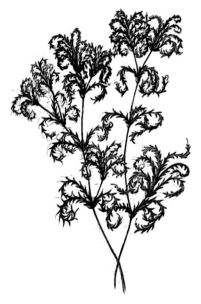

Najas minor.

Najas minor

This European annual aquatic (also known as Bushy Pondweed) has slender, narrow, light-green, curled leaves. It is propagated by seed. A North American species in the same genus, *N. microdon*, with tufts of transparent, olive-green leaves, is perennial and may be propagated from cuttings.

Potamogeton

A large genus containing over 100 species of submerged aquatic plants. Many of them are extremely fast growing and can quickly choke a pond unless constantly controlled. Species suited for colder areas include *P. crispus*, with oblong, wavy edged leaves and spikes of reddish flowers; *P. lucens*, with large, glossy elliptical leaves on stems which can grow several meters in length, and *P. natans*, with floating oblong leaves.

Ranunculus aquatilis

Also known as Water Crowfoot. A common, aquatic member of the buttercup family, *R. aquatilis* is a good oxygenator which will do well in small ponds, lakes or slow-running water. The submerged leaves are segmented while the emersed, often floating leaves are three-lobed. In the spring, a colony of *R. aquatilis* will produce a fine show of yellow-centered white flowers. Related species, also suitable for the ornamental pond, include *R. circinatus* and *R. flabellaris*.

Vallisneria

A genus of semi-hardy, grass-like plants favored by aquarists, as they are decorative, easy to grow, and make good oxygenators. The most commonly cultivated species is *V. spiralis*, with strap-like, semi-spiral leaves. The female flowers are borne on narrow spiral stalks which

Potamogeton crispus.

Vallisneria spiralis

break the water surface. The male flowers are borne at the base of the leaves and, when ripe, are released from the parent plant and float to the surface where they are ready to touch and pollinate the female flowers. Once fertilized, the spiral stems retract and the seeds ripen below the water surface. *V. spiralis* and the closely related *V. americana* may be propagated by detaching the runners which are freely produced. They are suitable for outdoor ponds in frost-free areas.

FLOATING FOLIAGE PLANTS

There are many reasons to have floating plants covering your water garden. They protect baby fishes, they keep the pond cool and algae resistant by protecting the water from the direct rays of the sun and the floating plants themselves are very attractive. Photo by Dr. Herbert R. Axelrod.

Planting water lilies in tubs keeps the top fairly clear so the colorful fishes are more visible.. The edges of the pond are planted with irises. Photo by V. Capaldi.

The plants in this category include those most decorative of all additions to the ornamental pool. The water lilies, in view of their importance, will be treated here in a little more detail than the other aquatics. The water lilies belong to the genus *Nymphaea*, which contains about 50 species of hardy and tropical plants, representatives of which grow wild in most countries of the world; the majority, however, are endemic to Africa and tropical Asia. Some species have been cultivated for thousands of years, and they are featured in wall drawings of ancient temples in India and Egypt. The ancient Egyptians were known to cultivate the lotus (probably *N. lotus*, the Nile Water Lily) and use both the seeds and the roots as items of food. The seeds were pounded and used for making bread, while the roots were eaten both raw and cooked. Many early writers refer to various parts of water lilies being used not only for food but also as aphrodisiacs, as medicines for treating such ailments as gout, dysentery and other bowel infections, and for religious purposes. In Australia today, aboriginal peoples still eat the leaves, fruit and tubers of *N. gigantea*.

In view of their beauty and aesthetic appeal, water lilies have been extensively cultivated in more recent times to produce hundreds of hybrids. The symmetrical star-shaped flowers come in an amazing range of colors ranging from white, cream or yellow through pink, red, orange and mauve to blue and bicolored. The blooms can vary in size from tiny individuals barely 2cm (3/4 in.) in diameter to enormous creations over 35cm (14 in.) across. They may be single, semi-double or double and may float on the water surface or be supported on aerial stems up to 30cm (12 in.) in height.

The father of hardy hybrid water lilies must have been the French botanist Joseph Bory Latour-Marliac (1830-1911), who in 1858 was stimulated into experimenting with this group of plants after reading an article by Professor G. Leveque in La Revue du Jardin des Plantes de Paris. In his article, the professor remarked on the beauty of certain exotic species and lamented the fact that they

were insufficiently hardy to be grown in the rivers and ponds of France. At that time, only the hardy European water lily *N. alba* was being cultivated outdoors, but Marliac soon began to import and experiment with exotic species.

At an early stage, a carmine-red mutation of *N. alba*, found in a lake at Neriko in Sweden, enabled Marliac to introduce pink forms of *N. alba*, *N. tuberosa* and *N. odorata*. The yellow Mexican *N. mexicana* was produced in hardy form in 1881 and was named "Marliacea Chromatella." Numerous cultivars were produced by Marliac between 1883 and 1890, and many of these were given the prefix "Marliacea" or "Laydekeri" (after Maurice Laydeker, his son-in-law). Marliac's hybridizing methods were kept strictly secret and

Nymphaea rubra devoniensis, a beautiful natural water lily.

unfortunately died with him. However, he enriched the world with some 70 varieties of hardy water lilies.

A great deal of the early work on tropical hybrids was carried out by the late George Pring at the Missouri Botanical Gardens in St. Louis, Missouri. He produced the first pure white cultivar "Mrs. George H. Pring" and later pioneered a great number of many colored tropical hybrids.

CULTIVATION OF WATER LILIES

Hardy water lilies are best planted directly into their outdoor pool in the spring or early summer. Although they may be planted directly into the substrate at the bottom of the pond, it is best to grow them in baskets so that you have easy access to them for removal for division, replanting or overwintering. Water lily baskets made from durable plastic are available

The universally preferred floating plant is the water lily. They can even be cut and used to decorate the inside of your home. There are hundreds of different kinds of water lilies. Photo by V. Capaldi.

from specialist nurseries. The holes in the mesh should be large enough to allow the root system to spread out into the surrounding substrate. Hardy water lilies have two kinds of root systems: one has thick central rootstocks with smaller roots spreading out at the base; the other has horizontally growing, banana-shaped tubers. The former must be planted upright in their baskets, the latter laid horizontally. The growth medium should consist of heavy garden loam containing about 15% of rotted cow manure, or about 250gm (half pound) of coarse bonemeal per basket. Special fertilizers for aquatic plants can be purchased from your suppliers. These may be added according to the manufacturer's instructions.

To help contain the planting medium in the basket, it should be lined with thin plastic sheeting into which a number of horizontal slits have been made to allow the roots to develop. Plant the tubers very firmly, leaving the crowns of the plants just above the surface of the planting medium. The top of the medium can then be covered with a 2.5cm- (1- in.) layer of well washed, pea-sized shingle, which will stop organic particles floating out of the medium and clouding the water and will also discourage fish from digging into the medium and exposing the roots. Hardy water lilies can be left outside all of the year in most climates, providing the rootstock is not subjected to freezing temperatures. However, in very cold climates the baskets should be removed from the

pond and the rootstocks placed in clean, damp sand in containers which are overwintered in a cool, dark place (garage or cellar, for example) where the temperature remains around 50°F.

Tropical water lilies are either grown in indoor ponds in temperate areas, or they are not planted outside until all dangers of frost are past. In Europe and the United States, this can be as late as June or July, depending on the climatic region. Of course, in the tropics, most of the subtropics, and selected temperate areas, they may be left outside throughout the year. Most tropical water lilies are started under glass at a temperature of around 68°F. Most of them have small, roundish tubers which are planted in small pots of sandy loam. When the leaves start to sprout, they are transplanted to their permanent baskets (without disturbing the root system) which contain growing medium as described above for hardy water lilies. The freshly planted roots should not be planted in deep water. Stand the baskets on bricks at first so that the crowns are just below the surface of the water and only lower them in gradual stages to the floor of the pool as vigorous new growth appears.

HARDY WATER LILIES

Nymphaea alba

This very hardy, robust species, known as the European White Water Lily, has leaves up to 30cm (12 in.) in diameter. The flowers are

10-12cm (4-5 in.) in diameter and are snow-white with yellow stigmas. Plant in 60-90cm (2-3 ft.) water depth. It spreads up to 0.75 sq meters (8 sq. ft.).

Nymphaea odorata
Known as the North American White Water Lily. The original wild species has bright green leaves and fragrant white flowers. A number of varieties are available.

1.

2. NYMPHAEA cv AURORA

3. NYMPHAEA cv PERSHING BLOOMING TROPICAL

4.

5.

6. NYMPHEA CAPENSIS VAR. ZANZIBARIENSIS

7.

8.

Nymphaea tetragona

This is a small, fairly cosmopolitan species. The olive-green foliage is pickled by the Japanese and placed on the menu. The small white flowers are about 5cm (2 in.) in diameter. Plant at a depth of 20-30cm.

Nymphaea tuberosa

This is a large species from the northeastern United States. The deep-green leaves are up to 45cm (18 in.) in diameter. The large white flowers are up to 20cm (8 in.) wide. Water depth 60-120cm (2-4 ft.), spread up to 0.5 sq meters (5 sq. ft.).

HARDY HYBRIDS

The following are just a few of the many hardy hybrid water lilies.

"Attraction" has large red flowers up to 20cm (8 in.) across. It should be cultivated at a depth of 60-90cm (2-3 ft.).

"Aurora" is a small hybrid requiring a water depth of 30-60cm (1-2 ft.). The leaves are mid-green, marked with reddish-brown. The pale yellow flowers, 5-7cm (2-3 in.) across, change to deep rose with age. Spread up to 0.2 sq. meters (2 sq. ft.).

"Conquerer" has dark green leaves up to 25cm (10 in.) across. The flowers are rose-crimson with red-streaked outer petals and about 15cm (6 in.) in diameter. Plant at about 60cm (2 ft.) depth. Spread up to 0.3 sq. meters (3.5 sq. ft.).

"Escarboucle" is probably the most brilliant red of all water lilies. The flowers are up to 20cm (8 in.) in diameter. The first flowers of the season may be white or red and white. The dark green leaves are up to 25cm across and the plant's surface spread is 0.25-0.35 sq. meters (2-3.5 sq. ft.). Plant at a depth of about 60cm (24 in.).

"James Brydon" is a small- to medium-sized hybrid with deep-pink flowers about 10cm (4 in.) across. The leaves are glossy-maroon at first, changing to dark green, splashed with maroon as they age. Plant at a depth of 30-90cm (24-36 in.). Spread up to 0.25 sq. meter (2.5 sq. ft.).

"Rose Arey" is a medium-sized water lily which should be grown at a water depth of 30-45cm (12-18 in.). The leaves are mid-green and the beautiful, fragrant flowers deep pink with yellow stamens; these are 10-16cm (4-6 in.) across and borne on stems several centimeters above the water level.

"Sunrise" is a medium-sized, strong growing, American hybrid which flowers profusely under warm conditions. The flowers are deep sulphur-yellow and the leaves mid-green, spotted with reddish-brown. Plant at a water depth of 30-45cm (12-18 in.).

TROPICAL SPECIES

All of the tropical species described here should be cultivated at temperatures of not less than 70°F in the summer and 50°F in the winter. All require a water depth of 25-45cm (10-18 in.) and have a spread of 0.3-0.5 sq. meters (3-5 sq. ft.). Some of the species and hybrids are viviparous, producing young plants at the center of the leaf where the stem terminates. These little plants can be used for propagation. Detach the plantlets and insert them in 3-in. pots of sand standing in warm, shallow water. They are then finally planted when three or four new leaves have appeared.

In the day-blooming species and hybrids, the buds usually open between 10 am and noon and close between 4 and 7 pm. The buds of the night-blooming varieties open at dusk and close sometime between dawn and midday. In most cases, the blooms do not float at the water surface but are borne on aerial fleshy stems up to 32cm (12 in.) above the surface. The flowers are usually strongly fragrant and last for three to five days either on the plant, or cut as vase specimens.

Nymphaea ampla

A prolific white flowered species from tropical America, the star shaped blooms are about 12cm (5 in.) across and stand well out of the water.

Nymphaea caerulea

This species, known as the Blue Nile Lotus, is widespread throughout northern and central Africa in suitable localities. The leaves are mid-green and wavy-edged. The fragrant flowers are pale-blue and mounted on long stems. The stamens are spotted with black.

Nymphaea capensis

This South African species, known as the Cape Blue Water Lily, has smooth, mid-green leaves which are red or pink on the underside. The star-shaped, light-blue flowers are very fragrant and 10-12cm (4-5 in.) across. They stand on stems up to 25cm (10 in.) above the water surface.

Nymphaea flammea.

Nymphaea chromatella.

Nymphaea J. Thimes.

This is the wild white water lily which is called Playboy at Rose Gardens.

The water lily Rosey Morn.

Photos by Joseph L. Thimes

Reddish water lilies proliferate and there are many varieties.
This common variety has no name.

Nymphaea flavivirens

This is an extremely vigorous Mexican species with fragrant, star-shaped, white flowers up to 20cm (8 in.) in diameter. The stamens are golden yellow.

Nymphaea gigantea

This magnificent species, known as the Australian Giant Water Lily, has large, sky-blue flowers up to 30cm (12 in.) across. The numerous incurved stamens are golden yellow. The leaves are green above, purplish beneath.

Nymphaea heudelotti

A rarely cultivated species from central Africa, bearing small bluish-white flowers 5cm (2 in.) in diameter.

Nymphaea lotus

This most famous of water lilies, known as the Egyptian Lotus, has thick, succulent roots and deep-green leaves with slightly ruffled edges. The night-blooming, matt-white flowers are up to 20 in. in diameter.

Nymphaea micrantha

A viviparous species, producing young plants from the foliage. The small bluish-white flowers bloom clear of the water.

Nymphaea rubra

A night-flowering species from India, having large reddish-brown leaves up to 45cm (18 in.) across and bright red flowers.

Nymphaea stellata

Native to India and Southeast Asia, this species has heavily fragrant flowers 20-25cm across. They are lavender-blue, with a golden yellow center. The sepals are green, speckled with black.

TROPICAL HYBRIDS

"Afterglow" is a bicolored hybrid with golden centered, orange-yellow and pink flowers.

"American Beauty" has large, wavy-edged, green leaves and red flowers with yellow centers up to 25cm (10 in.) in diameter.

"August Koch" is a viviparous hybrid which will bloom throughout the year in tropical or indoor conditions. The blue flowers reach 20cm (8 in.) in diameter.

"Bagdad" has green leaves blotched with chocolate-brown and short-stemmed blue flowers.

"B.C. Berry" is a night-blooming variety; the leaves have indented margins and the amaranth-purple flowers reach up to 25cm (10 in.) in diameter.

"Blue Beauty" was developed at the University of Pennsylvania. The deep blue flowers are up to 30cm (12 in.) in diameter and the golden stamens are purple tipped.

"Bob Tricket" has bright blue cup-shaped flowers reaching 35cm (14 in.) in diameter. The yellow stamens are tipped with blue.

"Daisy" is a viviparous hybrid with saucer-shaped, golden-centered white flowers. The green leaves are mottled with brown.

"Director G.T. Moore" has mid-green leaves and star-shaped blue-purple flowers with a yellow center.

"Emily Grant Hutchings" is a night blooming hybrid, with very large, cup-shaped, pinkish flowers.

"Frank Trelease" has large deep-crimson flowers up to 25cm (10 in.) in diameter; night blooming.

"General Pershing" has large pink flowers with pink tipped yellow stamens. The flowers are borne up to 30cm (12 in.) above the water surface.

"H.C. Haarstick" is a night-blooming form with copper-colored leaves and fragrant, deep-pink flowers held well above the water surface.

"Henry Shaw" has light-blue saucer-shaped flowers and light green foliage.

"Isabelle Pring" has very large green leaves and white fragrant flowers.

"James Gurney" has very large leaves with fluted margins and fragrant deep-pink flowers up to 25cm (10 in.) across; night blooming.

"Judge Hitchcock" has small mottled leaves which are purplish beneath; the cup-shaped, violet flowers are centered with blue-tipped, yellow stamens.

"Midnight" has numerous small flowers; deep purple with yellow centers.

"Missouri" has enormous blooms up to 35cm (14 in.) in diameter. The flowers are broad petalled, pure white and very prolific. The large, mottled leaves are indented at the margins; night blooming.

"Mrs. Edward Whitaker" has enormous pale lavender flowers over 30cm (12 in.) in diameter; the contrasting stamens are sulphur yellow.

"Mrs. George C. Hitchcock" is a night blooming variety with large deep-pink flowers and orange stamens.

"Mrs. George H. Pring" has large pure white flowers up to 35cm across.

Nymphaea laydekeri. Photo by Joseph L. Thimes.

"Mrs. Martin E. Randig" is a viviparous form with very large cobalt-blue flowers.

"Mrs. Woodrow Wilson" is a viviparous hybrid with large lavender-blue flowers and green foliage.

"O' Marana" has bright red flowers up to 30cm across; there is a faint white line running down the center of each petal; night blooming.

"Panama Pacific" is a very popular viviparous hybrid. The deep blue flowers develop reddish or purplish mottling as they age.

"Persian Lilac" has moderately-sized, lilac-colored flowers with pink-tipped, golden stamens; the small leaves are red beneath.

"Pink Platter" has large, rosy-pink, flattish flowers with pink-tipped yellow stamens. A viviparous hybrid.

"Rio Rita" has moderately-sized deep pink flowers with pink-tipped golden stamens. The small leaves are lightly speckled with maroon above and reddish beneath.

"St. Louis" was the first good yellow hybrid, produced by Pring in 1932. The very large star-shaped flowers are primrose-yellow with darker stamens.

"Sunbeam" is a viviparous hybrid with large sulphur-yellow flowers; the buds are striped with purple.

"Talisman" has small green leaves with reddish undersides; the star-shaped flowers are yellow flushed with pink.

"Wild Rose" is a viviparous form with large-petalled rose-pink flowers; the stamens are pink-tipped.

"William Stone" has large purplish flowers with an amaranth shade.

FLOATING AND MARGINAL PLANTS

Care should be taken in the use of floating plants in the ornamental pond. Under ideal conditions, many of them are extremely prolific and will soon completely cover the pond surface, cutting out light to the detriment of the other inhabitants of the pond. However, used discreetly and kept under control, certain floating plants are useful in supplying a certain amount of shade (and possibly food) for fishes, as well as adding aesthetic appeal to the whole concept. Most floating plants are cultivated by simply floating them on the water surface.

Ceratopteris (Floating Ferns)

A genus of succulent ferns with submersed or floating forms. They require temperatures of 68-72°F to proliferate. *C. thalictroides*

Ceratopteris thalictroides.

(water sprite) from Southeast Asia is probably the best known species. This has long, light green, deeply divided fronds, about 45cm (18 in.) long and 20cm (8 in.) wide. Plantlets are formed along the edges of fertile fronds and

these can be used for propagation.

Eichhornia crassipes (Water Hyacinth)

This is an attractive but invasive floating aquatic, introduced from South America to many tropical and sub-tropical parts of the world. Although not frost-hardy in temperate regions, it can be used outdoors as long as it is overwintered in a warm aquarium or greenhouse. The smooth

Eichhornia crassipes.

green leaves have bottle-like bases, containing air-filled spongy tissue which aids floating. The leaves form rosettes, from which spikes of purplish-blue, hyacinth-like flowers emerge. The purplish roots trail down into the water as much as 90cm (3 ft.). These form excellent refuges and breeding areas for fishes.

Hydrocharis morsus-ranae (Frogbit)

A European floating aquatic with rosettes of small, fleshy leaves about 2.5cm (1 in.) across. In the spring, white three-lobed flowers form on separate male and female

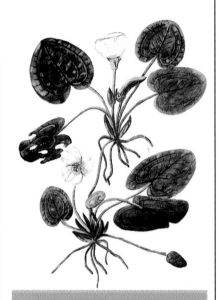

Hydrocharis morsus-ranae.

plants. It reproduces also by means of stolons, new plants forming at the ends. Dies down in the winter, new plants forming from buds which have overwintered in the mud. Not particularly invasive and a useful, hardy floater.

Lemna (Duckweed)

A genus containing a number of species of tiny floating plants which are extremely invasive, often covering the whole water surface, making it resemble a smooth green lawn. Due to its invasive habit, duckweed is regarded as a pest by many pond keepers, but kept under control it has its uses. It provides food and shade for goldfish and patches of it on the water surface can look most attractive. Excess weed can be fished out with a net at regular intervals.

Lemna minor.

Lemna minor has a pair of light-green circular leaves 2-3mm (1/8 in.) in diameter. Rootlets up to 1cm (1/2 in.) in length grow into the water from the center of the underside. It rarely flowers but reproduces vegetatively. Must be kept under control if kept in community with other plants.

MARGINAL PLANTS

Marginal plants are those aquatics which grow with their roots submerged in water but have emergent foliage and flowers. No informal pond is really complete without its marginals. These increase the natural impression by concealing the sometimes harsh edges to the pool. Many marginals are extremely ornamental, and some may provide shallow spawning and feeding grounds for your fishes.

Most marginals require fairly shallow water, so you must bear this in mind when constructing your pond. Shelves which will contain growing medium should be incorporated near the pond margins, so that the water depth above the medium does not exceed 10cm (4 in.). Alternatively, the plants may be contained in submersed porous pans, pots or baskets. A rich growing compost is not

Acorus calamus.

recommended, as foliage growth may become too lush at the expense of flowers. A good medium garden loam with maybe a little bonemeal added is usually ideal. The growing medium should be covered with a 2.5cm (1 in.) layer of fine shingle to

discourage fish from digging up the roots.

Acorus calamus (**Sweet Flag**)

This species originated in eastern Asia, but has now been naturalized to many parts of the world, including Europe and North America. Growing to a height of 75cm (30 in.), this plant is often mistaken for an iris as it has similar leaves and rhizomes. The brownish flowers, however, are more arum-like, being borne on short spikes at the tops of the stems. An attractive variety of this species has yellow striped leaves.

The closely related *A. gramineus* from China and Japan is a smaller species, dwarf and variegated varieties of which are often used in aquaria as submerged aquatics.

Alisma (**Water Plantains**)

A widely distributed genus of shallow water plants with plantain- like leaves and small tri-lobed pink flowers. *A. gramineum*, found in most of the northern temperate regions, has lanceolate leaves up to 50cm (20 in.) in length and 30cm- (12 in.-) long flower stalks. *A. plantago-aquatica*, the great water plantain, also from the northern temperate regions, is an extremely prolific species which must be kept under good control if it is not to take over the entire pool margins at the expense of other plants.

Calla palustris (**Marsh Arum**)

A native of north temperate and sub-arctic America and Asia, this species has also colonized various parts of northern Europe. It is a

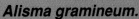
Alisma gramineum.

Calla palustris.

scrambling plant, ideal for masking pond edges. It has smooth, green, heart-shaped leaves produced from creeping rhizomes, growing to 25cm (10 in.) high. In late summer it produces small white arum-shaped flowers, followed by red berries. It is propagated by dividing the rootstocks and planting them in shallow water.

Iries at Sunken Gardens Park. Photo by Joseph L. Thimes.

Iris

This large, well-known genus includes a number of species suited to growing in shallow water. All may be propagated by division or from seed. *I. laeviata*, originating from Japan and Siberia, is one of the best known species and numerous varieties have been cultivated. The type species has smooth, green, strap-like leaves up to 75cm (30 in.) long and large, bright-blue, yellow-striped,

Nymphaea aquatica.

iris-like flowers. Varieties include "Alba," with white flowers; "Atropurpurea," colored rich violet; "Benikiren," being blue and silver; "Colchesteri," a blue-mottled white, and "Variegata," with blue flowers and cream-striped foliage.

I. pseudacorus, the European yellow flag, is another well-known species with sword-like leaves to 90cm (3 ft.) and large yellow flowers. Varieties include "Bastardi," with lighter yellow flowers; "Golden Queen," a richer yellow; and "Variegata," with yellow striped leaves.

Nymphoides

A genus containing a number of attractive aquatics useful for warmer ponds or aquaria. *N. aquatica*, from the southern USA, is often called the banana plant on account of its clusters of banana-shaped tuberous roots. It bears floating, roundish leaves up to 15cm (6 in.) across and small, violet-spotted, white flowers. *N. indica*, the water snowflake, of circumtropical habitat, is an attractive little plant with floating leaves and clusters of yellow-centered white flowers. *N. peltata* is the hardiest species; native to Europe and Asia, it grows in long strands with roundish, mottled purple, green leaves. It produces golden-yellow poppy-like flowers about 2.5cm (1 in.) across. Propagate all species by division.

Ranunculus lingua (Water Buttercup, Spearwort)

A European marsh plant growing to 90cm (3 ft.) in height and bearing lanceolate leaves and large buttercup-like flowers about 5cm (2 in.) across on many branched stems. Hardy and easy to grow in shallow water. Propagate by division.

Sagittaria (Arrowheads)

This genus contains aquatic and semi-aquatic plants, some of which are used extensively by aquarists.

S. montevidensis, the giant arrowhead from tropical America, grows to 75cm (30 in.) high and has large arrow-shaped leaves up to 40cm (16 in.) long. The large white flowers, borne on spikes, have purple spots at the base of their petals. Suitable only for frost-free areas or indoor ponds. *S. sagittifolia*, the European Arrowhead, is less spectacular but frost-hardy. The white flowers are borne on 45cm- (18 in.-) stems. Propagate by division of the tubers.

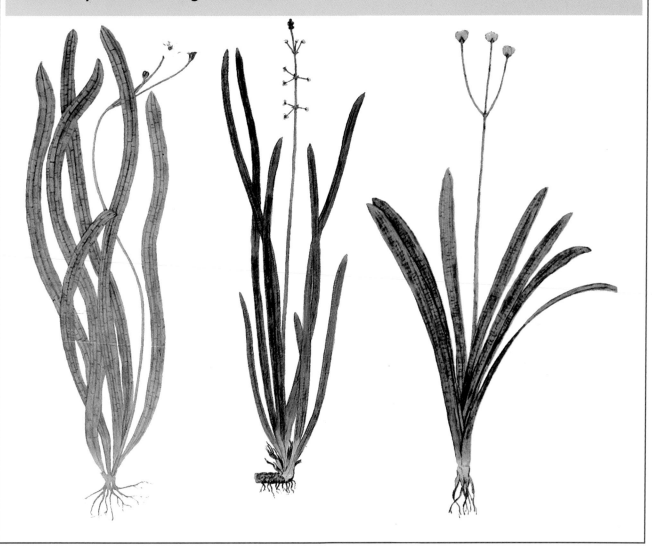

Three varieties of Sagittaria. **From left to right:** *Sagittaria subulata natans, Sagittaria subulata pusilla* **and** *Sagittaria teres.*

POND FISH AND OTHER ANIMALS

Some enthusiasts create a pond because they like fish, others because they are fond of aquatic plants; however the majority like to create an attractive water feature which has a balance of animal and plant life. Even when water gardeners do not deliberately introduce animals into their ponds, sooner or later the water will be teeming with a great variety of organisms. Many of these are microscopic, but others, such as water beetles, will fly to the pond from elsewhere. Insects with aquatic larvae, such as dragonflies, damselflies, mayflies, mosquitoes, etc., will lay their eggs in the ponds. The eggs of water snails and other aquatic invertebrates will be carried to the pond in the mud adhering to the feet of birds or the fur of small mammals— even native fish have been known to be introduced to ponds in this manner. Amphibians such as frogs, toads, newts, and salamanders may find your pond an ideal place to breed in the spring. Predatory mammals, birds or reptiles may visit the pond in search of food. All of these animals have a part to play in the ecological balance of a natural water feature but, in the small confines of the ornamental pond, some of them can become a nuisance, either devouring your plants or preying on your fish. It may be necessary to control some of the more unwelcome visitors.

Fish are the type of livestock one usually introduces into an ornamental pond. Although they are not strictly essential for the well-being of the pond, a pool without fish is like "strawberries without cream": they add that subtle "taste." There are also a number of advantages to having fish: they are attractive to look at and bring movement into your pool; they devour, and thus help control, other organisms, such as mosquito larvae and plant pests; and they help fertilize the aquatic plants with their excreta, as well as provide carbon dioxide from their respiration to aid photosynthesis.

There are several kinds of fish which can be kept in the outdoor pond.

GOLDFISH

The domestic goldfish was first developed by the ancient Chinese from red-tinted examples of native fishes closely related to the Crucian Carp, *Carassius carassius*. The common goldfish has the scientific name of *Carassius auratus*.

The original wild variety of *Carassius auratus* still occurs in the murky waters of sluggish streams in China today and is still sold as food in Chinese markets. The wild goldfish is somberly colored, but natural mutations sometimes occur which show patches of the characteristic red or gold colors of the domesticated varieties. It is not known exactly when the goldfish was first domesticated as an ornamental fish, but it is fairly obvious that the ancient Chinese bred these colorful varieties by selective breeding of mutant wild fish which showed patches of promising color. We know from literature that by the 13th century these fish were being bred commercially. In the 15th century, the goldfish found its way to Japan, where further varieties were produced. Goldfish first reached Europe in the 17th century and the USA about 100 years later. Today, the goldfish is to be found in almost every country in the world. The goldfish is hardy. Some varieties can live in the unheated outdoor pond all year 'round in most climates, providing there is sufficient depth to prevent the water freezing up completely. There are estimated to be over 130 recognized varieties of goldfish. Some goldfish are well suited to pond life, but some are not. Check with your dealer to make sure that the type you want to buy is suitable to your pond.

The Common Goldfish:

This is the fish of original shape and only its color differs from the wild type. It has a typical fish-form, is deep-bodied, has a wide, short head and a small mouth. The bright body scales may be gold, bronze, red or silver or a mixture of any of these colors, sometimes with patches of black or white. The dorsal fin begins at the highest part of the back and is relatively tall and slightly concave. The common goldfish is the hardiest of all the varieties and is highly suited to the outdoor pond. Those pond keepers requiring simple, trouble-free specimens are well advised to be content with this variety.

Common goldfish. Photo by Fred Rosenzweig.

Well-cared-for goldfish can reach a length of 30cm (12 in.) or more in suitable climates and can be expected to live in excess of 20 years.

The Shubunkin:

This handsome fish with matt scales was first developed in Japan at around the turn of the century. It was soon introduced into Europe and the USA. It resembles the common goldfish in shape, but its coloration is exceptional. The background color is often gray-blue and this is unevenly blotched and spotted with red, gold, brown and black. Several varieties of shubunkin have been developed in Europe, including the "Bristol" and the "London," both of which are similarly colored. However, the former has a higher dorsal fin and a longer tail, while the latter is more similar in shape to the common goldfish. Most shubunkin varieties are hardy

Shubunkin goldfish. Photo by Fred Rosenzweig.

and will thrive and breed in outdoor ponds. Young shubunkins soon assume adult coloration and, if adequately fed, will reach sexual maturity in one year. However, the young are rather delicate up to the age of about six months and should preferably be brought into indoor tanks or ponds for their first winter.

The Comet:

The comet goldfish was developed in the USA towards the end of the 19th century. A comet may be red, white or red and white in color and the scales are metallic. The tail fin

Comet goldfish. Photo by Fred Rosenzweig.

is as long or longer than the relatively slender body and the dorsal fin is deeply concave and tapered to a point at the rear end. This is an attractive, lively and hardy variety which will do well in the outdoor pool.

The Fantail:

This plump, oval-bodied fish is one of the older varieties which were introduced into Europe as early as the 17th century. It is one of the hardier of the fancy varieties and will live in the outdoor pond all year, providing the deeper water remains above the freezing point. The fish occurs in both metallic and matte versions, the latter often having the colors of the shubunkin.

Fantail goldfish. Photo by Fred Rosenzweig.

The outstanding characteristic of the fantail, as its name suggests, is the large caudal fin which has four lobes. The dorsal fin is high, the front edge being almost at right angles to the body. The ventral fins are rather large and the anal fins are paired. The fantail is a relatively short fish, rarely exceeding 8cm (3 in.) in body length.

The Veiltail:

The veiltail was developed in the USA from a mutation of the Japanese fantail. The paired caudal fins of this variety are about twice the length of the almost spherical body and should hang at an angle of approximately 45 degrees from the lateral line. The caudal fins are squared off at the rear as if they have been cut with a knife. The dorsal fin is high, often higher than the height of the body. Both metallic and

Veiltail goldfish with brocaded scaling. Photo by Fred Rosenzweig.

matt versions are available, the latter with shubunkin coloration. Veiltails are fairly delicate and should not be kept in outdoor pools where temperatures are likely to fall below 50°F. There is evidence to suggest that they require a greater amount of protein than most varieties and so should be given a considerable amount of live-food.

The Lionhead:

This is one of the more bizarre varieties. There is no dorsal fin and it has a strange, wart-like growth (the hood) covering the head. The growth usually appears when the fish is about four months of age but the quality of the growth depends, to a great extent, on the manner in which it is raised. The fish require individual attention and the young are best reared in indoor tanks. They are fed with tubifex and bloodworms (in considerable quantities) and water is kept free of algae. Both metallic and matt lionheads are available. Like the veiltail, the lionhead is more suitable for outdoor ponds in sub-tropical or tropical areas, as it is not hardy to excessively cold temperatures.

The lionhead goldfish has the growth on the head but no dorsal fin. Photo by Fred Rosenzweig.

The Oranda:

This variety has a body shape similar to the lionhead and it also has a warty growth covering the head, but this is more pronounced on the forehead. The hood matures when the fish is about 6 months of age. Unlike the lionhead, the oranda has a very prominent dorsal fin and the tail-fin is similar to that of the veiltail. Colors are variable and include combinations of red, orange, yellow, white, gray, black and blue.

The oranda goldfish has a growth on the head and a dorsal fin. Photo by Fred Rosenzweig.

The Pom Pom:

There are two major varieties of pom pom. The Chinese pom poms has the body of a lionhead and fleshy growths from the nostrils (sometimes referred to as narial bouquets) which move visibly as the fish swims. The Japanese pom pom has a body similar to that of the oranda and the pom poms are more elongate. Pom poms are only suited to indoor ponds or aquaria, or to outdoor ponds in warmer climates.

A red and black pom pom fantail goldfish. Photo by Fred Rosenzweig.

KOI

In the last two or three decades, the koi has increased tremendously in popularity as an outdoor pond fish. Koi are highly developed forms of the common carp, *Cyprinus carpio*, which is itself a relatively dull bronze-colored, bottom dwelling fish. However, the Japanese and others have developed a number of highly colored varieties which have an outstanding decorative effect in the ornamental pool. Koi are bottom feeding fish, more so than goldfish, and they produce large amounts of sediment in their feeding and defecating habits. Unless only two or three specimens are kept, or the pool is very large, a system of artificial filtration is essential with these fish.

Koi are extremely hardy and can grow to an enormous size. They will tolerate a high range of temperatures; however, an available water depth of 1.5m (5 ft.) is recommended for the larger specimens. There are many recognized basic varieties of koi and it is probable that many more will arise in the future, not only in their native Japan, but in Europe, America, and other parts of the world where the fish have become

A taisho sanshoku koi champion owned by Kiyoshi Sato.

universally popular. Most of the traditional varieties still have their original Japanese names and it will be prudent only to mention a few of the more colorful varieties here. Anyone requiring a deeper knowledge of koi is advised to obtain one of the specialist volumes available on these delightful fish. Some varieties of koi are: Asagi, white checkered with dark gray on upper surface, tinged with red or orange below and on the finnage; Doitsu Ogon, bronze or brownish, scaleless patches, but with rows of enlarged scales along mid-body and along the dorsal surface; Harawake-Ogon, plain, silky platinum colored;

Hikari Shiro-Utsuru, white or platinum base color, with black or dark gray patches; Kin Ki-Utsuru, marbled in red or orange and black; and Kawari-Mono, white or platinum base color, patched and spotted with red or orange and black.

GOLDEN AND SILVER ORFE

Next to goldfish and koi, orfe (*Leuciscus idus*) are probably the most popular fish for the ornamental pond. Both silver and golden varieties of this slender fish are available. They are active and very beautiful fish which spend much of their time near the water surface hunting insects, frequently leaping out of the water in pursuit of such prey.

The most popular color variety of koi is the two colored kohaku. This champion is owned by Kaneshige Yoshida.

Leuciscus idus.
Photo by W. P. & C. Piednoir.

TENCH

There are two varieties of this fish (*Tinca tinca*): the original green tench and the golden tench. They are not particularly valuable for ornamental purposes, as they spend most of their time at the bottom of the pond. However, a couple of these fish will make useful scavengers and they will cohabit amicably with goldfish.

THE RUDD

The wild rudd (*Scardineus erythrophthalmus*) is an attractive silvery gray with reddish fins, but there is also

The tench, *Tinca tinca.*
Photo by B. Kahl.

a golden variety in which the scales are the color of burnished bronze and the fins are deep red. They are an attractive shoaling fish for the ornamental pond and can be kept in community with other species.

**Carassius carassius.
Photo by B. Kahl.**

THE ROACH

Similar in appearance to the wild version of the rudd, the roach (*Rutilus rutilus*) is also a good shoaling fish for the larger ornamental pond, where it prefers well-planted areas.

CATFISH

Care must be taken when selecting species of catfish for the ornamental pond. Although they often make good scavengers, they are rarely visible once they are in the pond, and some of them reach an enormous size. Many a pond keeper has placed a few small catfish in his pond and they have "disappeared" only to reappear as monstrous, murderous specimens a couple of years later as they gulp down all the other ornamental fish in the pond!

FEEDING FISH

Some people erroneously believe that fish in an outdoor pool will be able to find all of their own food and therefore additional feeding is not required. Others tend to feed their fish too much, which results in uneaten food falling to the substrate, decaying and fouling the water. With regard to the first point, fish in outdoor pools can, and do, find a lot of their own food by nibbling at aquatic plants and eating aquatic insects and others which fall into the water. However, an ornamental pond usually carries a greater population of fish than would be found in a given volume of water in natural conditions, so additional feeding is required. Food for pond fish is available in convenient pellet form. These pellets are manufactured from a mixture of animal and vegetable matter and constitute a balanced diet; all of the essential proteins, fats, carbohydrates, minerals and vitamins are contained in them and, in theory, these are all a fish will need to keep it in prime condition. Care should be taken not to give the fish more food than they can comfortably consume in a few minutes each day. It is best to know your fish and to feed them individually with a few pellets at a time. This is a time-consuming but pleasurable task and much preferable to risking pollution.

As well as commercially prepared foods, a certain amount of live foods and other foods may be given. Earthworms chopped into small pieces will be taken greedily. Tubifex worms and daphnia, which can be purchased from aquarist suppliers, can also be occasionally given as a treat. If you intend to breed fish, live food is especially beneficial during the breeding season. Certain household items can also be given to your fish occasionally. Stale wholemeal bread crumbs can be given in small quantities, as can pieces of cooked vegetables, such as boiled potatoes, cabbage or carrots; chopped hard-boiled egg is also a valuable high-protein food. You can experiment with any number of household foodstuffs, but do not give fatty or oily foods. As with any food, on no account

This *Ictalurus* catfish typical of many types of catfish available for ponds and water gardens. They do stir up the bottom at times.

should you give more than can be comfortably consumed in a few minutes. It is better to throw the scraps away than to let them pollute the water in your pond.

As winter approaches and temperatures drop, the fish will stop feeding and become sluggish. This is the fishes' resting time when they go into semi-hibernation. In the temperate climates of the northern hemisphere, one should stop feeding the fish around the middle of November or as soon as ambient temperatures fall below 50°F. However, the fish must be well fortified to bring them through the winter rest period. During

The roach, *Rutilus rutilus*.

the late summer and fall, one should gradually increase the protein content of the fishes' food by giving more live food, meat, egg, etc. As soon as the fish start losing their appetites, as temperatures fall, cease feeding them altogether for the winter season; it is positively dangerous to continue placing food in the pool when it is not being consumed. Sometimes, on a bright, warm winter's day the fish may become active and swim near the surface, but you should not be tempted to feed them. If they are hungry, the sparse natural foodstuffs in the pond will tide them over. Indiscriminate feeding in the winter can cause digestive troubles and eventual death in the fish, as further cold temperatures will not allow the food to be digested and it may foul the system.

In spring, around the end of March, gradually start feeding the fish on a regular basis, with increasing amounts as the days become warmer. In April and May, at the beginning of the breeding season, the protein part of the diet can again be increased.

BREEDING FISH

Goldfish in a pond will usually breed naturally if you have males and females. During May to August (the breeding season in the northern hemisphere), much chasing about will occur, usually in the shallower parts of the pool. The object of this activity appears to be a desire of the male to bump the underside of the female with his snout in an endeavor to encourage her to release the eggs from her plump, gravid body. This mating activity usually takes place among thick clumps of water plants in shallow areas of the pond. If you want your fish to breed well, it is therefore essential to include shallow parts about 15cm (6 in.) deep at the margins, during the initial construction of the pond. When the female accepts the male,

Pet shops carry a variety of foods and special products for pond fish and other pool inhabitants. Photo courtesy of Ocean Nutrition.

she will begin to lay her eggs among the water plants. These are laid singly, each one being about the size of a pinhead. The sticky surface of the eggs allows them to adhere to the leaves of the water plants and, during this time, the male will be releasing milt to fertilize the eggs as they are laid.

If you are keeping your fish for aesthetic purposes only and are not breeding them for profit or exhibition purposes, you can let everything take its natural course in the pond. In reasonably warm temperatures, the fry will hatch in about 7-10 days; they are very small and appear like 1/8 in. slivers of glass suspended from the water plants. During the first few days they do not require extra food, as they will still be obtaining their nutrition from the yolk-sacs attached to their abdomens. After all of the nutrients from the yolk-sac have been absorbed, the fry become free-swimming. The pond will have sufficient microscopic organisms to sustain a fair quantity of fry and it is only when large numbers of fry are being reared in the aquarium that you will need to give them special fry-rearing food. You will not produce large numbers of young fish in the pond as the great majority of the eggs and fry will be lost to predators and adult fish which have no compunctions about devouring their own offspring or that of others. A few fry, however, will survive naturally, eventually growing to maturity and providing a continuance of fishlife in the pond.

Serious breeders of goldfish provide their fish with "spawning mops"—clumps of aquatic plants bound together, dried willow roots, or even nylon mops. Once the eggs are laid and fertilized, the spawning mops can be removed to an empty pond or tank for the rearing of the fry. The scope of this volume cannot comprehensively cover the serious breeding of pond fish species; enthusiasts interested in this branch of the hobby are advised to consult the specialist literature.

AMPHIBIANS

The class Amphibia includes the frogs, toads, salamanders, and newts, most species of which require standing water in which to reproduce. Everyone should be familiar with the life-cycle of the frog, which lays its clumps of eggs, enclosed in jelly-like capsules, in the water in early spring. These hatch into fully aquatic, gilled tadpoles which gradually metamorphose into lung-breathing frogs during the summer. Salamanders and newts have a similar life-cycle.

The fire salamander thrives in a standing water garden pond. It is scientifically known as *Salamandra salamandra*. Photo by K. Lucas.

It is surprising how soon a wild population of these creatures will set up home in a garden pond—even in the cities. Species will, of course, vary, depending on which part of the world you live in; but none of these fascinating creatures will do any harm in your pond and you will have the knowledge that you are doing your little bit for the conservation of species which are becoming scarce, even endangered, due to loss of habitat. In effect, by having a garden pond, you are replacing some of the habitat probably lost through development (i.e., land

Green frogs, or frogs like them, come and go. Photo by I. Francais.

reclamation of swampy areas, etc.). Most people tolerate the mating calls of frogs (often the first signs of spring), and the amphibians themselves are avid consumers of garden pests, so should be encouraged rather than maligned.

If you are not fortunate enough to attract a natural population of amphibia to your pond, you can introduce spawn from elsewhere: perhaps from the garden pond of an acquaintance, or from a natural pond (taking care that you are not contravening any wildlife protection laws). There is a good chance that adult amphibia metamorphosed from introduced spawn will stay in the area, especially if you provide cover for the adults. An increasing trend is to allow parts of the garden to revert to a natural state for the conservation of native species of plants and animals. If you have such an area in the vicinity of your pond, you will provide habitats for many species. Well-planted rockeries also provide good hiding places for frogs and salamanders.

REPTILES

The class Reptilia includes the snakes, lizards, crocodiles, and turtles. In general, reptiles, especially snakes, are less welcomed into the garden than amphibians. However, many small lizard species are welcome guests as, like amphibia, they feed on garden pests. In most parts of the world, the types of small water snakes that may visit or dwell near the garden pond are non-venomous and harmless to humans; however, they will make a meal of some of the frogs or newts in the pond, and sometimes even the fish! Most snakes are fairly sparse in numbers and are not likely to become a major problem in the garden pond; most will just take a meal and then disappear. In fact, some enthusiasts like to encourage the occasional water snake—it creates added interest to the pond which, if it is large enough and natural enough,

Thamnophis proximus. Photo by W. Mara.

should provide a balanced support for many forms of local wildlife.

Turtles are another fascinating addition to the garden pond but, unfortunately, turtles and fish are not compatible unless the pond is a very good size and you have a large population of the former and a very small population of the latter. Turtles will feed on fish, as well as other aquatic animals, and can

The toad-head turtle.
Photo by I. Francais.

soon clear fish from a small pond; if you want to keep turtles in a small pond, you will have to dispense with the idea of keeping fish in the same pond. Alligators or crocodiles are unlikely to be kept in a garden pond unless the owner is extremely eccentric!

INVERTEBRATES

Even if your pond does not naturally attract amphibians or reptiles, it will be certain to attract a veritable potpourri of invertebrate life which will set up home in and around the water. Useful pollinating insects such as bees, hoverflies, butterflies, and moths will visit the flowers. In addition, you will have your usual quota of plant-eating pests such as slugs, snails, caterpillars, and beetles, but these problems beset all gardeners, not only water gardeners!

The water will attract aquatic species such as water beetles. Some of the larger varieties can pose a danger to smaller fish, but if your pond is of adequate size and is carefully maintained, a harmonious balance will ensure no species is completely lost. In very small ponds, any predatory insect seen can be fished out with a net and destroyed before causing too much damage. Many insects have aquatic larval stages; these include mosquitos and midges, the larvae of which will be eagerly devoured by the fish. The predatory dragonfly has a larval stage which, if anything, is more ferocious than the adult, and larger species will catch and eat small fish. In such cases you can do little more than accept your losses, but with the comforting thought that you are doing your little bit for nature conservation.

Water snails will soon turn up in your pond, whether you put them there or not. The species (of which there are many) will depend on the area in which you live. However, most water snails are a benefit to the pond, rather than a pest, as long as they do not proliferate too greatly. A number will be eaten by the fish and other predators in the pond. Snails or their eggs may be inadvertently introduced with water plants, or they can be carried to the pond on the feet of birds. Although some snails actually eat the tissues of larger water plants, the majority browse on the algae deposited on the leaves and thus perform a service. Other species eat the sediment consisting of decaying plants, uneaten fish-foods and the excrement of other water creatures, thus assisting in the general recycling of waste. If you are unfortunate enough to have snail species which destroy your water plants, you can control them to a certain extent in the following manner: float a whole head of lettuce on the water surface in the evening; as water snails are unable to resist lettuce, they will congregate on it overnight in large numbers. The lettuce is then fished out and the snails destroyed. You can use the same lettuce several nights running and can continue the treatment until you reduce the snail population to an acceptable level; but do not use the lettuce once it has started to rot.

Freshwater mussels are useful animals to have in your pond. These are unlikely to arrive in the pond by themselves, but they may be purchased from some aquatic suppliers or collected from natural habitats. The species *Anodonta cygnea* is most usually available. Freshwater mussels are extremely good filters. Being filter feeders, they continually pass water through their systems, removing organic particles and using them as nutrients. They can completely clarify the water in a small pond in this manner. The mussels move about on the bed of the pond by using their projecting "foot."

A fish-eating water snake, *Neroda sipedon*. Photo by W. Mara.

GENERAL MAINTENANCE

Once a pond has been set up and a natural balance has been achieved, one should have surprisingly little maintenance chores to perform. The usual plant maintenance, such as pruning, thinning out, and replanting will be carried out in much the same way as in traditional gardening, but there are a number of extra points to bear in mind when dealing with a pond.

THE WATER

The quality of the water used in the pond may sometimes cause problems, but these are surmountable. By far, the majority of pond keepers fill and top off their ponds with tapwater. Although the water usually emerges from the tap as a clear fluid and is perfectly safe for human consumption, the quality of this water may not be the best for the plants and animals in our pond. First, most municipal water supplies are purified with chlorine, and a certain amount of free chlorine may still be in the water when it emerges from the tap. The small quantity of chlorine (usually measured in parts per million) is not dangerous to us but can have an irritant effect on animals and plants in their watery surroundings. In addition, the chlorine is added to destroy tiny, potentially pathogenic organisms in order to make the water safe for us to drink. The chlorine is not selective and will also destroy bacteria and other organisms which are essential to the natural balance of the pond. Fortunately, free

chlorine will soon disperse in standing water by combining with various materials to form insignificant quantities of relatively harmless chlorides. For this reason, when we fill our pond, it should not be stocked with fish or other animals until the water has "matured" (i.e., the free chlorine has dispersed, and colonies of bacteria have been allowed to develop). This maturing period should ideally be about one year after introducing the plants. However, most pond keepers will not have the patience to wait this long.

Various manufacturers of aquatic supplies have come up with ever more sophisticated ways of treating tapwater to make it quickly safe for pond life. Visit your supplier and ask his advice about available products, then use them to the manufacturer's instructions.

Secondly, the quality of tapwater also varies, depending on the area in which it is collected. Water from regions with bedrock containing lime will have "hard" water, while water collected from other areas will be relatively "soft." The hardness of water is an important factor for the garden pond; water which is too hard is not good for the pond's inhabitants. The overall hardness of water is due to the presence of dissolved salts (mainly those of calcium and magnesium), which the water picks up as it travels through

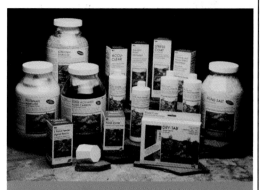

Many fine products are available for conditioning and treating water in a pond...very important considerations in the health of the pond's inhabitants. Photo courtesy of Aquarium Pharmaceuticals.

lime-containing bedrock. The more salts contained in the water, the harder it is. One of the most commonly used methods of measuring overall hardness is in degrees of German overall hardness (degrees GH or just GH). The GH can be measured by using a test-kit available from your supplier. There are several kinds of kits available, most of which work by adding an indicator solution to a sample of the water and comparing the water color produced with a color chart. Ideal pond water should have a hardness of 6-10 degrees GH. If the water is harder than 10 GH, you should attempt to reduce this hardness by adding clean rainwater to the general volume. Rainwater, however, often contains other potentially dangerous chemical compounds (particularly sulphates and chlorides), which have been absorbed from the atmosphere (usually as a result of man's industrial activities). For this reason, any rainwater used should be stored in a tank and treated.

Another factor which is important in the pond is the acidity or alkalinity of the water. The values of acidity or alkalinity will also depend on the amount and type of chemical compounds dissolved in the water and are measured on a pH scale. On the pH scale, the figure 7 is neutral (i.e., the borderline between acidity and alkalinity); the lower the number below 7, the more acid; and the higher the number above 7, the more alkaline. The ideal pH for most garden ponds should be between 6.5-7.5; around neutral. The pH value can also be measured with a test kit similar to the one used for testing hardness. You can regard pH levels below 6 and above 8 as being dangerous, and steps should be taken to buffer the water back to around neutral by using a special preparation available from your supplier.

ALGAE

The term algae collectively describes a number of uni-cellular plants which will soon populate any body of standing water. Algae are often misunderstood and treated as an evil presence; however, algae in a balanced form is essential to the natural ecology of the pond and thus to the well-being of its other inhabitants. Algae form the diet of many small creatures which in turn provide food for the larger ones. Like more advanced plants, algae also contribute to the gaseous exchange in the water through the process of photosynthesis. It is only when the algae become too rampant that they should be controlled.

Green algae is one of the first phenomena to arise in a new pond, particularly one in which the planting medium is too rich. In warm, sunny weather, the water will soon take on a green tinge as the algae reproduce and, in extreme cases, where the whole balance is incorrect, this can take on the appearance of thick pea-soup. These conditions are extremely dangerous to other plants in the pool, which will then soon die through lack of adequate light and carbon dioxide. The decaying plants will produce excessive toxins in the water which will, in turn, be a threat to the animal life in the pond. In addition, the algae itself will use up all the available nutrients and start dying off. In such cases, one will be left with a black, evil-smelling pool supporting nothing but anaerobic bacteria.

In most cases, however, the first green tinge to the water will soon go on its own accord, the plants will flourish, and the water will become crystal clear. To be on the safe side in the set-up stage, one can suspend small bags of black peat (these are available commercially from your supplier) in the water. The peat will decrease the pH of the water, making it less suitable for algal growth.

Suspended algae will also be inhibited if your pond has an adequate supply of submerged plants, as these will compete for the available nutrients. For emergency cases there are algicidal chemical preparations available, but these should be used with caution and only to the manufacturer's instructions.

Another kind of alga which can pose a problem is the filamentous alga commonly known as blanket-weed. This alga will thrive in good quality water and is not normally dangerous to the animal inhabitants of the pond, but it can choke water plants. It can normally be controlled fairly easily by removing batches of it with a garden rake. The use of suspended peat bags as described above will also help keep it under control.

PESTS AND DISEASES

In a well balanced pond, one is not likely to have much trouble with pests and diseases in the aquatic plants. Any invertebrates which attack plants are usually kept down to insignificant numbers by the fish and other predatory animals in the pond. The water-lily blackfly, *Rhopalosiphum nymphaeae*, can be a great nuisance, particularly in warmer summers when it breeds prolifically and soon covers the leaves and buds of many emersed aquatics, as well as water lilies. If left untreated, it will destroy the flowers and severely stunt the growth of the plants. Chemical treatment with insecticides is fraught with danger in garden ponds, as you will destroy not only the pests but also other invertebrates in the pond and possibly the fish. The best method of controlling blackfly is to forcibly spray the plants with water from a hose; the aphids will then be washed into the water and will be eaten by the fish and other predators. Another method is to forcibly hold the infested plants down under the water for 24 hours, by using hoops of wire or a system of weights.

The water-lily beetle, *Galerucella nymphaeae*, is another pest which can soon destroy your precious water lilies. Both the brown adult beetles and their fat black larvae eat holes in the upper surfaces of water lily leaves, which will eventually rot and disintegrate. These pests are most likely to occur at the peak of summer. They should be removed by forcibly spraying or submerging the foliage as described above.

Several species of moth of the genus *Nymphula* (china-mark moths) lay their eggs on water lilies and other aquatic plants. Upon hatching, the larvae bore into the leaves and stems. As they mature, they come out of the stems and will cut out pieces of leaves to form refuges for themselves, or curl leaves over for the same purpose. The caterpillars can be removed by hand and destroyed.

In general, aquatic plants remain surprisingly disease-free and most problems arise from incorrect conditions in the pond which can be alleviated by careful monitoring. Water lily leafspot is probably the most disfiguring disease to occur on our aquatic plants. There are several genera of diseases including *Cercosporae* and *Ovularia*, which affect the leaves with white or brown spots; these spread rapidly, eventually causing them to rot and disintegrate. Infected leaves should be removed and burned.

DISEASES AND PARASITES OF POND FISH

Like plants, fish will remain relatively disease-free if kept in ideal conditions. Diseases and parasites normally proliferate as a secondary effect after inadequate conditions have caused the animals to lose much of their natural immunity to attack. One of the first ways of ensuring that the fish in your pond remain healthy is to be certain that those you introduce into the pond are healthy in the first place. Buy fish from reputable suppliers only, and examine each one carefully before purchase. Do not buy fish which are thin or emaciated, which show any blemishes on the skin, or which have obvious eye defects. Observe the fish swimming and ensure that they are agile and orientated. Fish which are slow in reacting or swimming at any angle other than vertical are sick and must be rejected. In fact, if any fish in a container or holding tank show signs of a disease, it is good policy not to buy any of the inhabitants in the container. Go to another supplier or wait until the supplier has disease-free stock!

The safest way to avoid introducing fish diseases to an ornamental pond is to subject the fish to a period of quarantine before introducing them to a pond. The pond keeper should always have at least one tank for emergency purposes anyway. Although an all-glass aquarium tank is best for this, as it enables one to see the fish clearly, plastic garbage bins or similar articles can also be used. Ensure that you do not overpopulate a quarantine tank, and be sure to install an aerator of the type used by aquarists; use water from the pond in the quarantine tank so that the fish do not suffer too great a change when you transfer them. Other than the water and the aerator, no further furnishings are required in the quarantine tank, as these would only be in the way.

Precautionary disinfectants are available from specialist suppliers. Such a treatment can be added to the quarantine tank (according to the manufacturer's instructions). After seven days in the treated water, the water in the quarantine tank can be gradually changed with further water from the pond until by the tenth day the fish are again in pure pond water. The fish are retained in quarantine for a total of 14 days, after which they may be introduced to the pond, provided no disease symptoms become apparent. In such cases, the fish are retained in the quarantine tank and treated with the appropriate measures. Advice on fish diseases may be obtained from your aquarist supplier or from a veterinarian who specializes in fish diseases.

There are a number of fish diseases and parasites which may affect the fish in your pond. Unfortunately, it is not always easy to examine each fish in a pond individually. However, if you feed your fish regularly at the same spot in the pond, they will learn to come up for food and you will then be able to see if there are any serious problems. You will soon get to recognize individual fish by their characteristics and if, for example, a certain fish does not turn up for its meal, you can suspect there is something wrong.